Transforming the Gateway Course Experience

Serving as a call to action for educators to recognize and address inequities in gateway courses, this book offers an evidence-based model for improving teaching, learning, and student success within the foundational college classroom.

Gateway courses often reflect broader societal, cultural, and economic issues; this book argues that inequitable outcomes result from specific practices and policies, rather than occurring naturally. Using data and examples from his work with various colleges and universities, Andrew K. Koch highlights the systemic issues that perpetuate inequality in higher education. He examines how and why race and class divisions are reinforced through current practice and the impact that these courses have on students' sense of belonging. By giving suggestions for policy changes on how to combat high failure rates and challenging myths such as grade inflation and curve grading, this text seeks to critique and ultimately dismantle the toxic culture of "weeding out" students.

This accessible book is for any college instructor who wants to transform gateway courses into true opportunities for student success, ultimately advancing higher education's broader equity and social justice goals.

Andrew K. Koch is the Chief Executive Officer at the John N. Gardner Institute for Excellence in Undergraduate Education, Brevard, NC, USA.

"As I was sitting down to read Drew Koch's manuscript on *Transforming the Gateway Experience*, I was thinking that it would be a 'cookbook' or a 'workbook' on addressing what is a huge student success barrier in the universities and colleges around our nation. I have been in the student-success business almost 40 years and was extremely happy to see a scholar/practitioner put a pen to paper giving us some direction. What I got was that and much more. As I read this book, I became engrossed in the conceptual framework of his compelling argument which challenges us to 'put up or shut up.' Dr. Koch couched this call to action with historical knowledge and contemporary argument for why there is no time to waste if we believe that education is the great equalizer."

Aaron Thompson, *President, Kentucky Council on Postsecondary Education*

"Well-written, insightful, and compelling! Koch gets readers to think critically about our practices related to gateway courses, which are a critical aspect of student success. This is a must read for educators wanting to improve undergraduate education and ensure a socially just experience for all students."

Dan Friedman, *Assistant Vice President for University 101 Programs & the National Resource Center for the First-Year Experience and Students in Transition, University of South Carolina*

"Proponents of increasing student success in higher education should feel compelled to focus on courses, the building blocks of the curriculum, as the site for needed transformation. *Transforming the Gateway Course Experience: A Call to Action for Higher Education* describes compelling rationale and identifies tested tactics and proven maneuvers to equip leaders and disciplinary associations to act and plan for the constant nature of course redesign work at the gateway to the major—a site where too few students are welcomed into and supported to join the field and thrive."

Jillian Kinzie, *Associate Director, National Survey of Student Engagement (NSSE), Indiana University School of Education, Center for Postsecondary Research*

"Could there be a connection between college gateway courses and our nation's racial history? For Andrew K. Koch the answer is yes. Koch provides educators with eye-opening evidence that there is indeed a color line notably witnessed in DFWI grades in college gateway courses where the hopes and dreams of far too many racially minoritized students literally come to an end. Everything is in this book for educators to move away from adhering to myths about who can and can't succeed, as well as from what Koch calls tyrannical practices that do nothing more than perpetuate inequitable learning outcomes. This is the most promising book I have read that can truly change the futures of millions of students, especially those who remain underrepresented and underserved."

Laura I. Rendón, *Professor Emerita, University of Texas-San Antonio; Author of* Sentipensante Pedagogy: Educating for Wholeness, Social Justice & Liberation, *2nd Edition, Routledge, 2023*

"Transforming the Gateway Course Experience is a must-read for educators committed to transforming postsecondary education. The book highlights the critical role of gateway courses in student success, exposing systemic inequities and offering practical solutions. Key takeaways for me include the importance of addressing readily accessible data, fostering a sense of belonging, and implementing evidence-based teaching practices across curriculum. This book provides a roadmap for transforming educational outcomes and advancing equity in higher education."

Mac Powell, *President, Accrediting Commission for Community and Junior Colleges (ACCJC)*

"Transforming the Gateway Course Experience should be required reading for postsecondary educators of all types, full stop. Dr. Koch's contribution brings a combination of quantitative analysis and relatable institutional examples to clarify the issues and link them to two important underlying dynamics: the role of gateway courses in influencing student sense of belonging, and the ever-present 'weed-out culture mentality.' Most critically, he presents a clear, three-phase plan to dramatically improve the student (and faculty) experience, resulting in greater and more equitable outcomes."

Patrick Methvin, *Director of Postsecondary Success at the Gates Foundation*

"This is a significant, urgent, challenging, and practical book. Drew Koch draws on a vast dataset to demonstrate that those of us who teach and lead in higher education are largely responsible for persistently high student failure rates in introductory courses, particularly for students of color and first-generation or low-income undergraduates. Koch then shows us how we can change—individually and institutionally—to enable more students to learn and thrive in gateway courses, which is an essential step towards success in college."

Peter Felten, *Executive Director, Center for Engaged Learning, Elon University; Co-author, Connections Are Everything: A College Student's Guide to Relationship-Rich Education (2023)*

"*Transforming the Gateway Course Experience* is a must-read for anyone seeking to understand the significant role that gateway courses play in reproducing inequity and elitism in postsecondary education. Koch captures the systemic issues that have led to gateway course failure broadly and provides evidence-based alternative approaches that can be widely adopted."

Stephanie Sowl, *Program Officer, ECMC Foundation*

Transforming the Gateway Course Experience

A Call to Action for Higher Education

Andrew K. Koch

Routledge
Taylor & Francis Group
NEW YORK AND LONDON

Designed cover image: Getty Images

First published 2025
by Routledge
605 Third Avenue, New York, NY 10158

and by Routledge
4 Park Square, Milton Park, Abingdon, Oxon, OX14 4RN

Routledge is an imprint of the Taylor & Francis Group, an informa business

© 2025 Taylor & Francis

The right of Andrew K. Koch to be identified as author of this work has been asserted in accordance with sections 77 and 78 of the Copyright, Designs and Patents Act 1988.

All rights reserved. No part of this book may be reprinted or reproduced or utilised in any form or by any electronic, mechanical, or other means, now known or hereafter invented, including photocopying and recording, or in any information storage or retrieval system, without permission in writing from the publishers.

Trademark notice: Product or corporate names may be trademarks or registered trademarks, and are used only for identification and explanation without intent to infringe.

Library of Congress Cataloging-in-Publication Data
Names: Koch, Andrew K. (Andrew Karl), author.
Title: Transforming the gateway course experience : a call to action for higher education / Andrew K. Koch.
Description: New York, NY : Routledge, 2025. | Includes bibliographical references and index.
Identifiers: LCCN 2024032586 (print) | LCCN 2024032587 (ebook) | ISBN 9781620369623 (hardback) | ISBN 9781620369630 (paperback) | ISBN 9781003444961 (ebook)
Subjects: LCSH: Education, Higher—Curricula—United States—Evaluation. | Education, Higher—Aims and objectives—United States. | College teaching—Social aspects—United States. | Academic achievement—Social aspects—United States. | Discrimination in higher education—United States. | College dropouts—United States—Prevention.
Classification: LCC LB2361.5 .K64 2025 (print) | LCC LB2361.5 (ebook) | DDC 378.1/990973—dc23/eng/20240913
LC record available at https://lccn.loc.gov/2024032586
LC ebook record available at https://lccn.loc.gov/2024032587

ISBN: 978-1-620-36962-3 (hbk)
ISBN: 978-1-620-36963-0 (pbk)
ISBN: 978-1-003-44496-1 (ebk)

DOI: 10.4324/9781003444961

Typeset in Palatino
by Apex CoVantage, LLC

Contents

Foreword – Isis Artze-Vega and Jessica Williams ix
Preface. xiv
Acknowledgments. xviii

1 On Gateway Courses and DFWI Rates—Defining the Issues 1

2 The Gateway Course Completion Line 18

3 On Belonging—The Case for Learning Mindsets, Metacognition, and Faculty as Teaching and Learning Experts. 39

4 Weeding Out the Weed-Out Culture. 62

5 Taking Action—A Three-Phase Model for Gateway Course Redesign. 83

Afterword—Where Do We Go From Here? – Betsy O. Barefoot and John N. Gardner 122
Index 126

Foreword

One of us experienced the first year of college as the first time she felt completely seen, heard, and understood in the classroom, imbuing her with the confidence that she could succeed. The other recalls large, impersonal lecture halls and invisible expectations that effectively weeded her out of her chosen STEM pathway. Yet somehow, decades later, our varied professional experiences have led us both to wholeheartedly share Drew Koch's conviction that the time has come for higher education practitioners to focus our time and effort on gateway courses. In *Transforming the Gateway Course Experience: A Call to Action for Higher Education*, Dr. Koch does what he is uniquely positioned to do as a historian, the head of an organization that has been a national leader in gateway course reform, and someone who has spent countless hours supporting and learning from practitioners across the country: He places gateway courses in the spotlight—and at times, under a microscope—deepening our understanding of their impact on our students and institutions and providing invaluable, practical guidance for those of us ready to heed his call.

The mere existence of this book is noteworthy. Dr. Koch is the first scholar-practitioner to devote this much attention to the topic of gateway courses in higher education. His reflective, analytical approach in *Transforming the Gateway Course Experience* results in an honest, nuanced portrait of gateway courses that advances our thinking at several levels. At the macro level, for instance, Dr. Koch explores why so many gateway courses function as academic gatekeepers and attributes the status quo to what he calls the "tyranny of practice" and a "weed-out culture." He also debunks myths such as the perspective that students simply change majors when they are not successful in a gateway course and that they find pathways more suitable to their abilities. We are confronted with the reality that students' experiences in gateway courses correlate strongly to their retention. Far too many students leave our institutions altogether with their college hopes and dreams deferred. At the micro level, the text delves into unexpected, insightful particulars. Among them, the implications of grading on a curve and of "DFWI" (representing the grades of "D" and "F," withdrawal, and incomplete) rates, shedding light on the consequential nature of the oft-ignored and misunderstood course withdrawal "W" and incomplete "I."

Dr. Koch is also careful to provide readers with a multifaceted argument for transforming gateway course experiences. Like us, some readers may be compelled by the data on persisting differences in gateway course completion associated with students' identities, as well as by the parallel he draws between Jim Crow segregation and students' gateway course experiences. Others may find the enrollment- and bottom line-based rationale more convincing. Ultimately, as Dr. Koch explains, the significant demographic shifts in the U.S. higher education landscape mean that students' gateway course success is more urgent and vital than ever—for everyone. The American Council on Education recently reported that there has been a decrease in the share of White students from 65.9% in 1999–2000 to 47.6% in 2019–2020, indicating that nearly half of the undergraduate population now comprises students of color (Kim, Soler, Zhao, & Swirsky, 2024). As students of color continue to become a larger proportion of the prospective student pool and the majority of enrolled college students, institutions that do not attend to gateway course reform will find themselves replicating privilege and hemorrhaging enrollment.

As longtime higher education professionals, we see evidence of Dr. Koch's claims and of the importance of this work in our past and current roles. One of us (Dr. Williams) is deeply involved with a national organization that supports institutions in removing structural barriers to student success. Through this work, it is evident how persistently high DFWI rates in gateway courses, often stemming from poorly designed academic and support structures, can hinder student progress and negatively impact student outcomes. She finds that institutional leaders often lack the access to data needed to provide timely support to students, as well as systems in place to effectively use data to improve course outcomes, reinforcing the book's guidance on data collection, use, and supporting structures. Meanwhile, Dr. Artze-Vega has led gateway course-specific initiatives at two institutions (one, high research; the other, a community college). In both contexts, analyses identified a set of gateway courses for which performance predicted students' persistence. In some cases, as many as half of the students who received an unsuccessful grade (DFWI) did not enroll at the institution in the subsequent term. As a result of the extraordinary efforts of the Florida International University faculty and staff as part of its Gateway Project, improved course passing rates, compared to the baseline year of 2013–2014, have resulted in more than 40,000 instances of successful course completion, all while maintaining or elevating intellectual rigor.

Turning to two specific features of Dr. Koch's text, the presentation of data and case-making about the role of faculty are each commendable. While you engage with the comprehensive data throughout *Transforming the Gateway Course Experience*, you will no doubt be struck by the patterns and the factors that, time and again, predict students' gateway course success. Yet we invite you to also notice a more subtle characteristic of Dr. Koch's presentation of data—that it avoids the all-too-common phenomenon of "gap gazing," by which we mean identifying and making commentary on gaps in achievement among demographic subgroups, often with judgment and without context. Instead, he delves into the history of the gaps in gateway course completion, recognizing they are the legacy of systemic racism and classism. The integration of quantitative analysis and rich historical context reveals how policies, practices, and socio-economic conditions have systematically disadvantaged certain groups. This approach allows for a more complete understanding of the educational landscape, emphasizing that creating a more equitable and just educational system requires addressing structural impediments to success. At the same time, Dr. Koch does not let us off the hook. He balances the recognition of the structural context in which we operate with reminders of our agency and personal responsibility. By pointing to examples of others who have successfully transformed gateway courses, he demonstrates that improvement is both necessary and achievable.

On Dr. Koch's focus on faculty, he urges us to engage faculty as leaders and support their professional development as a core feature of gateway course transformation. We couldn't agree more and wonder, in fact, why the student success movement has not yet sufficiently focused on the role of faculty. The text describes why faculty and their teaching are so consequential to students' gateway course experiences, and Dr. Koch tackles head on the perception that increasing gateway course success necessitates inflating grading or simply "passing" students. He therefore counsels his readers to have initial discussions with faculty centered on learning and the extent to which students are meeting the course learning objectives. These discussions might also benefit from a bit of learning science—specifically, the fact that learning depends on prior knowledge (Lovett et al., 2023). In this way, gateway courses are not only significant because they can determine whether students stay enrolled, but they are also sites of critical, foundational learning upon which students must build in their future courses.

After four years of seemingly endless disruptions and changes in higher education—including declining enrollments and public trust and, relatedly, financial instability—Dr. Koch's book is a timely gift to our community. Given multiple goals and initiatives, in an increasingly competitive landscape, it can be hard to know what to prioritize. This book assures us that transforming gateway courses is a worthy focus and gives us a roadmap for success. All the while, he's honest with readers. This work will take significant time and energy, and we can expect that it will elicit defensiveness and suspicion. In addition to his candor, we appreciate that, as a White man with an established national platform, Dr. Koch recognizes his privilege and uses it to amplify the voices and experiences of marginalized communities. He shows a true commitment to allyship and advocacy, particularly in his understanding of the systemic barriers that have historically marginalized Black students and other underrepresented groups in higher education. Finally, we echo the optimism and sense of possibility underscored in *Transforming the Gateway Course Experience*. The examples in the text and our own professional experiences illustrate that equitable student learning and success at scale are indeed possible. Together, we can transform gateway courses from their historic role as gatekeepers to authentic invitations for students to join academia as their whole selves, grow and learn, and enrich our institutions with their innumerable strengths.

Isis Artze-Vega, *College Provost & Vice President for Academic Affairs, Valencia College, Orlando, FL*

Jessica Williams, *Senior Director of Client Service Delivery, National Institute for Student Success, Atlanta, GA*

References

Kim, J. H. J., Soler, M. C., Zhao, Z., & Swirsky, E. (2024). *Race and ethnicity in higher education: 2024 status report.* Washington, DC: American Council on Education.

Lovett, M. C., Bridges, M. W., DiPietro, M., Ambrose, S. A., Norman, M. K. (2023). *How learning works: Eight research-based principles for smart teaching* (2nd ed.). Hoboken, NJ: Jossey-Bass/Wiley.

Preface

This book is about what happens on the academic beachheads known as gateway courses. But it is also about the broader societal, cultural, economic, historical, and other factors that combine to make these introductory courses the perfect lens for examining what is or is not working well in the contemporary student success movement. Gateway courses also bring to light what is possible if we care enough to address issues in these courses and the broader systems and structures of which they are a part.

"Just try not to depress everyone." That is the guidance my wife, Dr. Sara Stein Koch, often conveys as I walk out the door on the way to give an address or conduct a workshop on gateway courses. Obviously, there is humor in her advice. There is also truth. The fact of the matter is the outcomes I share in those addresses and in this book can be quite depressing. If you are an educator who cares deeply about your students, these outcomes should also be maddening. And they should impel you to act.

As you read this book, you will notice that I tend to include historical, philosophical, and other forms of contextualization in the chapters that comprise this book. This is because, at my core, I am an American Studies historian, and that is what scholars like me do. That shared, I am an American Studies historian who focuses his research on education—particularly higher education and how colleges and universities shape and reflect democracy and culture in the United States. So, while this book is written by an American Studies "type," it is intended for postsecondary educators of all types. It includes a bit of history throughout because everything has a history, and that history shapes the present, and if not considered, continues to shape the future whether we like it—or are even aware of it—or not.

I did not create the conditions that I describe in this book. But I am compelled to, as James Baldwin once wrote in a 1962 essay in *The New York Times*, "speak out about the world as it is." While Baldwin was writing about the work of novelists, his guidance is equally applicable to educators writing about education. Baldwin asserts, "The effort to become a great novelist simply involves attempting to tell as much of the truth as one can bear, and then a little more" (Baldwin, 1962). This is the case with gateway courses in colleges and universities in the United States today. The inequitable outcomes in gateway courses, and the societal inequalities they help uphold, will not go away if we refuse to acknowledge them. Acknowledging these outcomes then requires us to act.

Intended as a call to arms for transforming gateway courses, this book is written in a somewhat informal style, using as much evidence as possible while keeping it accessible—a book than can be read over the course of a day or a weekend. I'll share examples from work that my Gardner Institute colleagues and I have done with hundreds of colleges and universities over more than twenty-five years. There are no fictitious persons or events shared in the pages that follow. What I share is the truth as my work has shown it to be—a truth that exposes a history of inequity in the many small practices that add up in big and deleterious ways in gateway courses. I also share a model for transforming gateway courses and guidance on how to implement that model, so that these courses can truly be gateways to future student opportunity and success.

I've worked in higher education for slightly over thirty years. I've held instructional, student access and success, enrollment management, and/or academic affairs roles at a variety of universities. Now, as I write this preface in 2024, I am a full-time employee of the non-profit John N. Gardner Institute for Excellence in Undergraduate Education—an organization focused on improving teaching, learning, and student success in higher education and, in the process, advancing higher education's broader equity and social justice goals. I've been fortunate to work at the Gardner Institute since 2010, serving as its chief executive officer since 2021.

Recently, I was struck with the realization that I am at a midpoint in my work and life. The first time that thought occurred to me, I was a bit surprised—because it arrived without any form of existential crisis. No impulse to buy a sporty red convertible, no sudden need for Botox. Despite the lack of existential angst, my fiftieth birthday gave me an opportunity for reflection—a chance to both look back and also look forward to the future. And not just my own future. This book commits to some directions for my work in the years to come—and more importantly, why those aims are important for society and its institutions at large.

Overview of Contents

The first chapter of the book, titled "On Gateway Courses and DFWI Rates," makes the case that gateway course failure rates need to be examined—in both aggregate and disaggregate—even if many members of the academy might find such an exploration distasteful, at least at the onset. The chapter defines gateway courses themselves, and the broader issues surrounding them. When considering the weight of the evidence, that chapter makes the case that course failure rates, like climate change, are very much "man-made" as opposed to "naturally occurring," and then goes on to suggest some ways in which practices and policies can and must be changed for the betterment of the students, colleges and universities, and the communities of which they are a part.

In the second chapter of the book, "The Gateway Course Completion Line," I point out how long-standing race and class divisions in the United States are being upheld through unquestioned practices and policies used in gateway courses at many colleges and universities today. The assertions are supported by data from thirty-six colleges and universities in the United States—a dataset that includes over 1.5 million student records. The manners in which gateway courses often reinforce stereotypes and convey exclusion—and how those messages fall more often than not on the ears of students from historically underrepresented and underserved backgrounds—are explored, as are approaches for altering this dynamic.

The third chapter, "On Belonging," sets up the broader narrative around how gateway courses send students message about whether or not they belong both in a specific program of study and in higher education altogether. These messages can be subtle, and perhaps even unintended. But they can reinforce preexisting stereotypes and feelings of inadequacy and close the doors for the exact students who increasingly will comprise the twenty-first-century postsecondary learner demographic.

Chapter four, "Weeding Out the Weed-Out Culture," addresses the weed-out culture that is pervasive in and at the heart of much of the toxicity traditionally associated with gateway courses. I take on myths and questionable practices such as grade inflation, curve grading, and the protection of "standards" that are used to thwart change and better outcomes in foundational courses and higher education broadly.

The fifth chapter, "Taking Action," provides an evidence-based three-part model that institutions have used to significantly improve teaching, learning, and success in gateway courses. As I noted at the outset, this book is a "call to arms." But it would be irresponsible to call readers to arms without pointing to a proven approach for change, and this concluding chapter does exactly that.

I hope the book will be read by educators of all types—faculty who teach, staff who facilitate learning, and administrators who bear responsibility for making sure that educational systems truly serve today's students. Each of us can help to transform gateway courses.

Reference

Baldwin, J. (1962, January 14). As much truth as one can bear. *New York Times Book Review*, 14, 2.

Acknowledgments

This book is more than a personal project. It is, in fact, a communal undertaking. I owe a great deal of gratitude to that community for making this book possible. On one level, I am reluctant to name the people who made this work possible—for fear of accidentally leaving someone out. On the other hand, there are several people whom I must publicly acknowledge—for, without them, I would have never written this.

First, I wish to thank John Gardner and Betsy Barefoot for over thirty years of mentorship and encouragement, and, in regard to this book, for prompting me to undertake the effort, reminding me to make time to write, and weighing in on my thinking all along the way. Betsy's "What do we need to do to make sure you get this book done?" question posed tactfully but persistently during the far-too-many-to-count lunches over the past five years and John's "You'll finish that book someday, right?" nudges were as necessary as they were nurturing. I also need to thank my colleagues at the Gardner Institute, whose immeasurable forms of support and patience allowed me to stay on top of a more-than-full-time job while also writing this book. Specifically, I need to thank Stephanie Foote, Betsy Griffin, Vicki McGillin, Rob Rodier, Brandon Smith, and Angie Whiteside—all Gardner Institute staff—as well as Gardner Institute Fellows Chaouki Abdallah (Georgia Tech), Isis Artze-Vega (Valencia College), Joshua Caulkins (Embrey Riddle University), Bryan Dewsbury (Florida International University), Peter Felten (Elon University), Casey Green (Campus Computing Project), Greg Heileman (University of Arizona), Mays Imad (Connecticut College), Susannah McGowan (Georgetown University), and Matt Pistilli (Iowa State University). In particular, I want to thank and point out the support from my long-time colleague and dear friend Brent Drake, who after years of service to higher education at Purdue University and the University of Nevada Las

Vegas recently joined the Gardner Institute as a full-time senior vice president. His data analysis skills and dexterities as a "loyal critic" made this book much better than it would have been if left to my own devices. I also need to thank my Gardner Institute colleague and partner in many projects Alicia Morey. Her diligence and support were the key ingredients that allowed me to finish this writing project on time.

I must also convey deep gratitude and appreciation to the Gardner Institute's board of directors, two members of which—Dr. Isis Artze-Vega and Dr. Jessica Williams—wrote the foreword to this book. Members of the board routinely reminded me how important it was to share what you find in this book. As Dr. Aaron Thompson reminded me, speaking on behalf of the board, "The higher education community needs to hear from you, Drew."

David Brightman, my "critical editorial friend," must also be publicly thanked. His candor about what "worked" and what did not—"Drew, I like history, but please don't bring in irrelevant stories about the Gallipoli campaign!"—and his encouragement when I was wrestling with whether events beyond my control made the book even relevant—"Drew, the book is an important contribution, and will have an impact beyond the days of the global pandemic"—kept me going when I needed inspiration and focused when I needed shepherding.

Alex Andrews and Kyanna Nusom at the Routledge/Taylor & Francis Group, this book's publisher, took what I wrote and what others helped me refine, and made it shine. I am grateful to Alex for taking me under her wing, checking in just enough to make sure I know she and the publisher wanted this book, but not enough to be annoying. The Routledge team is to be credited for helping me make this publication a reality.

Many of the lessons learned in this work were learned through projects supported by several national higher education-focused foundations and/or through conversation with staff affiliated therewith. Particular thanks go to Nazeema Alli, Nitasha Beri-Kumar, Russell Cannon, Archie Cubarrubia, Kelly Deforrest, Johannes de Gruyter, Francesca Mazzola, Patrick Methvin, Rupal Nayar, Bree Olofson, and Rahim Rajan, who inspired and supported me through the work they did or still do at the Bill and Melinda Gates Foundation. Similarly, I owe deep gratitude to current and past Lumina Foundation staff members Amber Garrison Duncan, Haley Glover, Jasmine Haywood, Debra Humpreys, and Nicole McDonald, as well as current or past staff members at The Kresge Foundation Caroline Altman Smith, William Moses, and Chera Reid. Current and former staff at the Ascendium Foundation who shaped my thinking and encouraged this book include Sue Cui, Amy Girardi, Bethany Miller, Rebecca Villarreal, and Keith Witham. Finally, ECMC Foundation colleagues Lynn Alvarez, Sarah Belnick, Stephen Handel, Stephanie Sowl, Peter Taylor, and Saúl Valdez also merit thanks for supporting the Gardner Institute's gateway course redesign efforts that influenced what I included in this book. Collectively, these philanthropic leaders' long-term interests in and commitment to the course redesign cause made this book a far better informed and personally fulfilling writing project. I just hope these persons find what I have done at least remotely as thoughtful and rewarding as the inspiration and intellectual stimulation they have provided to me over the years.

Support from these philanthropic organizations sustained, and continues to assist, Gardner Institute course redesign efforts with hundreds of institutions and thousands of educators across the United States. Those educators—faculty, staff, administrators, and in many cases students—have not only taught me a great deal about the "what and the why" behind gateway course but served as a constant source of motivation for my work.

I would be remiss if I did not also thank Shirley Malcom (American Association for the Advancement of Science) and Elaine Seymour (University of Colorado Boulder) for their willingness to respectively talk—and share wine, cheese, or potato chips—with me over the past ten years. The time they invested in my questions and thinking made me certainly feel like I had something to share—and what I share is better because of their investment. Also, I would like to thank Julia Brooking, Brendan Gillis, and Jim Grossman from the American Historical Association (AHA) for their ongoing engagement with my Gardner Institute course redesign efforts that have informed this work, as well as Edward Ayers and Annie Evans, with New American History, for the questions they asked and the encouragement they provided for the history-based inquiry that informed this work.

Also, thanks to the many higher education-focused publication editors who encouraged me to submit essays, published them, and then gave me permission to draw on those writings to write this book. These kind and inspirational souls include the aforementioned Jim Grossman, Executive Director of the AHA, and Emily Swafford, formerly with the AHA and now with the University of Michigan, who insisted that I write the essay "Many Thousands Failed" for *Perspectives on History*; James Rhem, from the National Teaching and Learning Forum, who cultivated and disseminated my essay "Big Inequity in Small Things" in his publication; and Thomas Bartlett, with the Chronicle of Higher Education, who encouraged, refined, and published my essay "Don't Weed Students Out. Help Them Flourish." Their respective and collective efforts helped me refine my thinking and arguments that I have expanded on for purposes of the book you are now reading.

Finally, and most important of all, I must thank my dear wife, Dr. Sara Stein Koch, and my six children—Andrejs, Maks, Hunter, Hudson, Grayson, and Lauren—for everything they did to make it feasible for me to work on this book. Whether it was time, patience, good humor, cajoling, or even kitchen table space, none of this would have been feasible without them. Their encouragement and love were the fuel I needed to get this book across the finish line.

I am indebted to all these people, and undoubtedly many others, for all that they provided over the past twenty-four months. The book is far better for what they have done. Its deficiencies and limitations are all mine. I only hope that what I have been able to do with the input and help from so many fine thinkers will, in turn, help fine thinkers at colleges and universities across the United States—and beyond—rethink what they are or are not doing to help students—particularly historically underrepresented and underserved students—learn more in gateway courses and succeed in them at higher rates than before.

1

On Gateway Courses and DFWI Rates—Defining the Issues

In 2023, while I was still working on this book, our society was wrestling with how the Supreme Court's "colorblind" ruling on two affirmative action cases applied to higher education. While reading the news coverage, I could not help but observe that most students of color are enrolled at institutions that look and operate nothing like Harvard or the University of North Carolina. In 2023, at most colleges and universities in the United States, race, ethnicity, and family income were the best predictors of who gets to graduate, not who gets in. Access alone does not guarantee equitable success. Yes, it is an imperative that educators and society at large focus on who gets in the collegiate front door. But it is also essential that we focus on who crosses the finish line. And that leads to the focus of this book: the oversized role that gateway courses play in determining who gets to graduate.

This chapter introduces a topic that the general public largely does not follow—a topic that makes many of those who teach college courses generally bristle, and a topic considered the "academic third rail" by many higher education administrators. It is about DFWI rates in foundational-level "gateway courses"—also known as "weed-out" or "gatekeeper" courses—and what those rates tell us, if we are willing to look, about systemized inequity and a climate of exclusion that manifests itself in and through gateway courses.

DOI: 10.4324/9781003444961-1

While seemingly obscure to some (most of the general public), and an irritating hot button topic to others (some, if not many, members of the faculty), DFWI rates cannot be ignored. Admittedly, they are, at best, rough proxies for what was or was not learned in the course. But DFWI rates can reveal some very disturbing trends about contemporary higher education—trends that can do irreparable harm to students and the colleges and universities they attend. To fully appreciate the issue, we must define the phrases "gateway courses" and "DFWI rates" and clarify how and why the various components of the DFWI rate matter.

Gateway Courses Defined

The definition for "gateway courses" used here is from a national project called Gateways to Completion (G2C), developed with my colleagues at the John N. Gardner Institute for Excellence in Undergraduate Education (Koch & Foote, 2018). The goal of G2C is to improve teaching, learning, and student success in historically high failure rate, high enrollment, gateway courses and, in the process of doing so, advance more equitable and socially just outcomes in undergraduate education. This occurs through the creation and implementation of evidence-based course redesign plans—plans that are informed by disaggregated data and centered around inclusive and active pedagogies.

As of Fall 2018, over sixty-five postsecondary institutions enrolling over 1.5 million undergraduates had been involved in the G2C effort. The G2C participating institutions included ten associates/community colleges, nine baccalaureate/associates colleges (four-year institutions that primarily grant associates degrees), six baccalaureate colleges, twenty masters colleges and universities, seventeen doctoral universities, and one institution outside the United States not classified by the Carnegie classification system. Naturally, with institutions coming from such varied sectors of higher education, my colleagues and I had to establish and then refine an appropriate, sector-spanning definition for the term "gateway course." The definition was generated through the help of a National Advisory Committee of over thirty-five postsecondary institution leaders, scholars of teaching and learning, faculty, institutional researchers, and student success leaders. It has since been applied in work at the nearly six dozen colleges and universities involved in the G2C process, and it has held up in the efforts that thousands of faculty and staff have undertaken in conjunction with the work. In other words, the definition you are about to read has been shaped by the collection and analysis of a lot of evidence, and tested and refined by the experiences and wisdom that come from a lot of practice.

Just as my colleagues and I did in our work at the Gardner Institute, I have made a conscious choice to use the phrase "gateway course" for this book as opposed to the commonly used "gatekeeper course" or "weed-out course" designations. Simply stated, names matter. And to say that this book is about "weed-out" courses directly implies that students who fail the courses are the academic equivalent of undesirable and troublesome plants. As the late American poet Ella Wheeler Wilcox wrote, "A weed is but an unloved flower" (Wilcox, 1911, p. 80), and as this chapter and the rest of the book shows, these courses, and their students, need a great deal of love and attention if higher education institutions are to live up to their stated values and approved missions. With these thoughts on nomenclature shared, for purposes of this chapter and book, a gateway course is defined as any course that is foundational, high-risk, and high enrollment in nature (Koch & Rodier, 2014). And now I share a bit more on each of those three defining elements.

Gateway Courses Are Foundational

Foundational courses may be non-credit-bearing developmental education courses—which often serve as "gateways" to the gateway courses—and/or college credit-bearing, generally introductory courses like introduction to psychology, introductory rhetoric and composition, U.S. history, college algebra, principles of accounting, introductory calculus, and so on. However, they can also be courses offered at a later stage in the undergraduate experiences that have a winnowing effect on the students who take them. Examples of this second type include microbiology and "A&P" (anatomy and physiology) that nursing students may take in the later stages of their second year or early in the third year of study.

Gateway Courses Are High-Risk

High-risk is measured by the rates at which grades of D, F, W, and I are earned across sections of the courses. I'll explore how we define those grades and DFWI rates a bit later in this chapter. It must be noted that we do not set a threshold for these grades in our work at the Gardner Institute—even though we are routinely asked questions like, "What DFWI rate makes a course high-risk?" My colleagues and I have been unwilling to do this because we firmly believe there is no universal rate that marks when a course is or is not high-risk. Context truly matters. And, quite frankly, if all students are demonstrating mastery and performing at exemplary levels, none should be receiving a D, F, W, or I grade. Thus, the rate that constitutes "high-risk" should be discussed and defined in local institutional settings by faculty and administrators involved in course redesign work. For reasons explained later in this chapter, discussions about "high-risk" courses and the grades that serve as metrics that they are high-risk should use both aggregated and disaggregated data for the courses, as a lot can be hidden in an aggregate DFWI rate.

Gateway Courses Are High-Enrollment

What constitutes a high-enrollment course is determined by the number of students enrolled within and/or across sections of the course as well as the context in which the resulting course enrollment number is compared and contrasted. "High-enrollment" can mean a large number of students enrolled in one section—such as a single section enrolling hundreds of students at a research university or an online institution. It could also mean many sections of a course each with smaller enrollments that add up to big numbers—such as twenty sections of English composition with twenty students enrolled in each section at an independent, residential, liberal arts college with a total student body of 800 undergraduates. In that environment, that course enrolls half of the institution's students. This means that an institution with 800 undergraduates would not use the same threshold for defining their gateway courses as a large institution with ten to 100 times that enrollment.

In my experience, all institutions have courses that enroll significant numbers of their students—whatever that number is. Many of these courses in turn, present challenges to the students who take them. As alluded to above, the challenge is measured, at least in part, by rates of D, F, W, and I grades—also known as the DFWI rate. The next section of this chapter defines and explores what those DFWI rates truly mean—and how that meaning challenges all postsecondary educators to change the status quo about what happens in gateway courses.

DFWI Rates Defined and Contextualized

Properly understanding the issues at work within gateway courses requires postsecondary educators of all types to unpack the DFWI rates associated with each of these courses. I have found through my work with faculty and staff from hundreds of colleges and universities that few topics can as quickly divide postsecondary educators as the topic of DFWI rates. A few years ago, when discussing the topic with a new chief academic officer, she expressed that she would be "a one-year provost" if she encouraged her faculty to examine and redesign high DFWI rate courses. I've known academic leaders who have had grievances filed against them by unions for pursuing work analyzing high DFWI rate courses. Others have had claims about what they supposedly said about DFWI rates led to embarrassing and potentially untrue reports in the national higher education media.

It is my firm belief that those who quickly dismiss the value of considering DFWI rates do so, at least in large part, because of lack of understanding about how the rates are derived, what each of the components of the rates truly mean, and the effect that earning the grades that constitute the DFWI rate has on students, particularly those from low-income and historically underrepresented backgrounds. What follows is an attempt to address that knowledge gap, with the hope that this knowledge can be applied by caring educators to change "weed-out courses" into catalysts for deeper learning and completion—also known as gateways to completion.

The "D" in the DFWI rate is representative of all D grades or their equivalent. In our work at the Gardner Institute—where we have been collecting and studying DFWI rate data from over 400 colleges and universities as part of our efforts since 2005—we include any kind of D grade, D+, D, and D−, in the calculation of this rate. On a 4.0 grade scale, this generally means course grades ranging from 0.7 to 1.3. Contrary to what some may believe, the D does not stand for course drops prior to the start of the withdrawal period—at least not in our work. This is because course drops prior to the withdrawal period *do not* factor into a student's grade point average and also *do not* get recorded on the official transcript.

The "F" in the DFWI rate is the designation used for a failing grade in a course. Some institutions use other designations for course failures—such as a Y. But, for purposes of comparison and computation my Gardner Institute colleagues and I equate any failing grade—meaning a grade that equates to a 0.0 on a 4.0 scale—to an F.

The "W" grade is representative of any form of withdrawal that is officially on the transcript. This includes withdrawals for medical reasons, withdrawals indicating that a student was passing the course when he or she withdrew (often a WP or a plain W), withdrawals that indicate that the student was failing the course when she or he withdrew (often a WF), withdrawals for disciplinary reasons, and so on. Unlike course drops before the withdrawal period, W grades *do* appear on the transcript. I have often heard colleagues dismiss the W grade—even claim that it should not be factored into the DFWI rate since it results in no true grade consequences. But this argument misses a key point. Even though Ws do not factor into the grade point average as a course grade, they still carry consequences.

Specifically, by being on the transcript, and thereby indicating that a student did not earn credit for a course he or she attempted, W grades "count" in the manner that colleges and universities calculate "Satisfactory Academic Progress" or "SAP." All postsecondary institutions that receive and distribute Title IV financial aid funds must use the Federal Department of Education's guidelines to determine SAP for their aid recipients. While the Department of Education leaves it up to each college or university to determine the exact manner in which SAP is interpreted and enforced, essentially a student has to successfully complete at least 67% of all credits attempted, and he or she must meet a minimum grade point average requirement (generally a 2.0 after a certain point in their academic careers) in the process of doing so (U.S. Department of Education, 2018).

Failure to meet SAP requirements results in the student no longer being eligible for Title IV federal financial aid programs—specifically the Pell Grant, Perkins Loan, Supplemental Educational Opportunity Grant, work-study, and direct student loans. In many states, the same SAP guidelines that apply to federal aid monies also apply to state financial aid funds. Note that the majority of the programs listed are grant or loan programs that support students from low-income backgrounds. This means that Ws do count—and they are especially significant for those students who can least afford to pay for college. In short, students who come from affluent backgrounds may be able to earn as many Ws as possible without worrying about financial aid eligibility. Poor students can't. Often, low-income students do not realize this until it is too late. And neither do many of their instructors—some of whom may actually encourage students to withdraw from courses without realizing the implications of doing so.

Like the W grade, the I grade—for incompletes or the institutional equivalent thereof—is also often dismissed by many who question the validity of DFWI rates. But, also like the W grade, the I grade carries deleterious implications and consequences. Some view the I grade as an intent to successfully complete the course. But often, intent does not mirror reality. As the policies from institutions as varied as LaGuardia Community College (2018) and the University of California at Berkley (2018) illustrate, "Incomplete" grades have short life spans—generally ranging between one semester to one year following their initial posting on the transcript. At the American Public University System, the student has thirty days to complete the I grade (2018) if he or she is not granted an extension by a faculty member. Across the vast majority of colleges and universities in the United States, the I grade automatically converts to a permanent F grade when it is not completed during the period allowed. At some institutions, such as Washington and Lee University (2018), students may no longer register for courses if they surpass a specific number of I grades. And as the University of Georgia Office of Student Financial Aid notes on its website, "One or more 'I' grades can adversely affect the Minimum 67% Pace of Completion component of *Satisfactory Academic Progress (SAP)*" (2018). In short, like the W grade, I grades matter—and often in ways harming the SAP and grade point average.

It is one thing to understand the grades that constitute aggregate DFWI rates and why those grades all matter and should be included in the calculation. However, *what truly exposes the inconvenient truth about DFWI rates are the findings when those aggregate rates are disaggregated by various demographic populations.*

With the help of Dr. Brent Drake, vice provost for decision support at the University of Nevada Las Vegas and a Gardner Institute fellow, and with the support of my colleagues at the American Historical Association, in May 2017, I published an essay in *Perspectives on History*, titled "Many Thousands Failed: A Wakeup Call to History Educators" (Koch, 2017). The essay shares the results of an analysis of DFWI rates in introductory U.S. history courses in thirty-two colleges and universities across the United States. One of the key findings of the study is that race and ethnicity, income, and first-generation status were directly correlated with who does or does not succeed in introductory U.S. history courses at the institutions in the study. For example, African American students have a DFWI rate that was nearly double that of their Caucasian/White counterparts in this course (42.37% for African Americans compared to 21.36% for Caucasian/White students).

Another key finding in our study was that the rate of failing a course as measured by DFWI grades—especially for students in otherwise good academic standing—was directly correlated with decisions to not return to the institution at which the course was taken. For example, students who were retained at their institution had a 19.27% DFWI rate in U.S. history. Students who were in otherwise good academic standing, meaning they had a grade point average of 2.0 or higher, but were not retained and elected to leave of their own volition had a 42.87% DFWI rate in U.S. history. In other words, earning a DFWI in perhaps even one course can be directly correlated with not returning to the college or university at which that grade was earned. When the previously mentioned demographic outcomes from the study are considered in connection with these retention findings, it should not be surprising that students of color as well as low-income and first-generation students have significantly lower college retention completion rates than their more affluent, non-first-generation, and/or Caucasian/White counterparts. What is surprising is that students don't seem to be flunking out—they are in good standing otherwise. Based on emerging research on student sense of belonging, growth mindset, and stereotype threat, the students may feel like they are being pushed out. This same body of research shows what we can do to increase a sense of belonging and reduce perceived threat, all the while maintaining if not enhancing course rigor (Aronson et al., 2009; Claro, Paunesku, & Dweck, 2016; Dweck, 2008; Yeager & Walton, 2011). That is, what we can do if we care. And there is reason to care. As the late Clifford Adelman's research shows, once students who do not succeed in even 20% of their courses leave college—and 20% of a course load could be just one course during the first term—they are unlikely to finish a degree not just at the institution where they earned the grade, but anywhere (1999, 2006).

For those who might take solace in the fact that these findings are for introductory history, I must share some more disturbing news. Dr. Drake and I are in the process of finalizing a report for seven other introductory courses—principles of accounting, general biology, general chemistry, English rhetoric and composition, college algebra, introductory college calculus, and general college psychology. A table summarizing some of the findings to be shared in that broader report is found in the second chapter of this book—so you can verify what I am about to convey by looking at some data. While the DFWI rates may vary by course, the trends are the same regardless of discipline. Students from groups historically underrepresented in and underserved by colleges and universities in the United States are those who are most likely to earn a D, F, W, or I in the foundational-level courses we are studying. Race, income, and both social and cultural capital truly matter. And, as will become abundantly clear in the second chapter of this book, race and ethnicity *really* matter.

This is the point in the chapter where I must make it abundantly clear that the solution to this issue is not to "give everyone an A." Far from it. But I have to make that point because, when in conversations about and sharing similar content on the topic of DFWI rates in the past, this is usually the stage when at least one person will defensively, exasperatingly, and perhaps even indignantly offer the response, "So then you just want me to pass everyone." This is quickly followed by "You want me to lower my standards!" To be clear, inflating grades or rewarding lack of effort do nothing to actually help students become future contributors to society and the workforce. Watered-down educational experiences don't mitigate inequity—they perpetuate it. But using the guise of "rigor" "or standards" to terminate even the start of a conversation about the meaning of DFWI rates does nothing either. In fact, these arguments about the maintenance of standards are essentially about maintaining the status quo—a status quo that means students from poor and historically underrepresented backgrounds pay the same tuition fees as their more affluent counterparts, only to fail at higher rates. This means that the poor and historically excluded are being asked to fund colleges and universities so that the latter do not need to do anything different. As a result, higher education could very well be contributing to the establishment of a permanent undereducated underclass—students that leave campuses feeling defeated and with education loan debt.

Evidence-Based Practices to Help Address the DFWI Issue in Rigorous and Equitable Ways

Faculty are right to be suspicious of the use of aggregate DFWI rates as a singular measure of their teaching performance. That is a blunt and totally inappropriate approach. However, when examined in both aggregate and disaggregated manners, contextualized with other forms of evidence about teaching and learning, and considered with evidence-based methods that have been studied and increasingly disseminated through the scholarship of teaching and learning over the past decade-and-a-half, DFWI rates are a metric that cannot be dismissed or ignored. They are useful metrics in helping teams of faculty and administrators identify, implement, and refine evidence-based practices in their courses—practices that deepen learning and, in turn, increase the successful attainment of the credentials that students are seeking when they enroll in gateway courses.

One form of evidence-based practice is what Arendale defines as peer-assisted/cooperative learning programs. There are many forms of peer-assisted/cooperative learning programs, but all of them "employ a student to facilitate or lead study groups for historically-difficult courses" (Arendale, 2018). Through an extensive literature review, Arendale has identified and categorized seven types of peer-assisted learning programs. They include (a) Accelerated Learning Groups, (b) Emerging Scholars Programs, (c) Peer-Assisted Learning (PAL), (d) Peer-Led Team Learning, (e) Structured Learning Assistance, (f) Supplemental Instruction, and (g) Video-Based Supplemental Instruction (Arendale, 2017). My personal preference is for any kind of peer-assisted/cooperative learning that is embedded into a course—since this means that it is not optional and that all students must be part of it. An example of a very successful peer support program is Nevada State College's Course Assistant initiative

(Koch, Prsytowsky, & Scinta, 2017; Nevada State College, 2018). This kind of effort puts support directly into the classroom, so that work schedules, stigma, or simple lack of knowledge about how college works are not reasons for students missing out on the benefits of supplemental learning.

Evidence-based, active learning strategies have also been shown to significantly improve student learning and, as a result, success. As Scott Freeman and his colleagues from the University of Washington noted in their meta-analysis of 225 active learning studies in the *Proceedings of the National Academies of Sciences*, "If the experiments [considered in the study] had been conducted as randomized controlled trials of medical interventions, they may have been stopped for benefit—meaning that enrolling patients in the control condition might be discontinued because the treatment being tested was clearly more beneficial" (2014). Particular forms of active pedagogies—such as inclusive pedagogies used by Bryan Dewsbury at the University of Rhode Island (Dewsbury, 2018; Field, 2018) or transparent pedagogies promoted by Mary-Ann Winkelmes (University of Nevada, Las Vegas, 2018)—have been shown to help all students, especially those with the least social and cultural capital, learn more and succeed at higher rates.

Other institutions have noted that many of their introductory sections are taught by part-time, adjunct instructors. This practice means that often the newest and least connected students who enroll in gateway courses are being taught by instructors who themselves are not well connected to the institutions and whose development as instructors is not supported by their employer. Florida International University (FIU) recognized this dynamic as part of the problem in several of the seventeen gateway courses it moved to redesign as part of its strategic plan to improve student success (Florida International University, 2018). As part of the effort, FIU hired and developed a cadre of instructors in several of the gateway courses it redesigned. While not tenured or on tenure-track, the instructors are multi-year employees with annual salaries and benefits. As part of their employment, the instructors are expected to adopt evidence-based pedagogies that help more students learn and ultimately succeed. The University invests resources in this professional development activity.

The facts that many graduate programs do not teach their students to use these strategies and that many institutions do not disseminate data and support their faculty in the application of that evidence to improve teaching and learning cannot be ignored. Freeman Hrabowski, longtime president of the University of Maryland-Baltimore County and chair of a National Academies panel that issued a report in 2010 about the lack of diversity in the STEM workforce, pointed out in an interview that much of the issue in the STEM fields lies in the way foundational courses are taught (National Academy of Sciences, 2011). He could have been talking about all disciplines, not just those in the STEM fields.

Hrabowski went on to explain that when faculty find challenges in teaching today's students, "(t)hey assume the students who fall short are simply not well-prepared," which he says is true for some students, but not really as many as thought. Hrabowski pointed to the growing body of literature and evidence about ways in which courses can be more effectively taught, but then shared that "many faculty don't have the time, resources, or institutional support to try anything new" (Mervis, 2011, p. 1333). The lack of support for practices and policies that enable, encourage, and reward faculty course redesign efforts is a systemic failure. In such a context, it should be little wonder that instructors, in turn, systematically continue to fail students.

Faculty are also frequently not taught about the students who will be coming to college in the years ahead—how the "majority-minority" status that the nation will attain in 2044 is already reality in many of the nation's elementary and secondary schools, and how that diverse enrollment is now "knocking at the college door" (Bransberger & Michelau, 2016). As a result, and as implied by Hrabowski, instructors are often overheard wishing for "better students," not knowing that "better" correlates with the dwindling number of White and/or affluent learners. But ignorance should not be tolerated as an excuse—especially not in institutions of higher learning that otherwise eschew ignorance in all its guises.

Changing the Weed-Out Climate

In summation, the current situation in gateway courses is a perfect storm. Many instructors view with suspicion and object to efforts that bring up DFWI rates in gateway courses. Administrators fear to tread into the DFWI rate discussion—out of concern about ugly battles and even votes of no confidence. Students are confronted with classes that are taught in ways that reinforce a sense of inferiority and encourage them to leave, to be weeded out of a discipline. With steadily changing demographics, these dynamics combine to create an environment that fosters more failure than success—especially for students of color, from poor families, and who are first in their family to go to college. Clearly, changes in gateway course environments must occur—before our instructors, institutions, and most importantly the students they serve, reach the point of no return.

I hope this chapter compels readers to accept the possibility that something bigger is at stake when DFWI rates are dismissed out of hand. Doing so allows the gateway course status quo to remain unquestioned and unchecked. DFWI rates are one of several measures that must be considered in a more nuanced and disaggregated ways and in conjunction with other forms of evidence and support. Doing so may very well reveal that introductory courses are perpetuating inequitable educational outcomes that may have started before students came to college but that can be reversed if educators are both empowered *and* care enough to act.

References

Adelman, C. (1999). *Answers in the tool box. Academy intensity, attendance patterns, and bachelor's degree attainment.* Washington, DC: U.S. Department of Education.

Adelman, C. (2006). *The toolbox revisited: Paths to degree completion from high school through college.* Washington, DC: U.S. Department of Education.

American Public University System. (2018). *Incomplete grades (extensions).* Retrieved from http://www.apus.edu/student-handbook/your-academic-success/your-course-grades-and-apus-transcripts/incomplete-grades-extensions.html

Arendale, D. (2017). *Postsecondary peer cooperative learning programs: Annotated bibliography*. Minneapolis, MN: University of Minnesota College of Education and Human Development.

Arendale, D. (2018). *Resources for peer assistant learning (PAL) programs*. Retrieved from http://arendale.squarespace.com/peer-learning-resources/

Aronson, J., Cohen, G., McColskey, W., Montrosse, B., Lewis, K., & Mooney, K. (2009). *Reducing stereotype threat in classrooms: A review of social-psychological intervention studies on improving the achievement of Black students (Issues & Answers Report, REL 2009–No. 076)*. Washington, DC: U.S. Department of Education, Institute of Education Sciences, National Center for Education Evaluation and Regional Assistance, Regional Educational Laboratory Southeast.

Bransberger, P., & Michelau, D. (2016). *Knocking at the college door: Projections of high school graduates* (9th ed.). Boulder, CO: Western Interstate Commission for Higher Education.

Claro, S., Paunesku, D., & Dweck, C. S. (2016). Growth Mindset Tempers the Effects of Poverty on Academic Achievement. Proceedings of the National Academy of Sciences, 201608207.

Dewsbury, B. (2018). Retrieved from https://blogs.scientificamerican.com/voices/the-soul-of-my-pedagogy/

Dweck, C. S. (2008). *Mindset: The new psychology of success*. New York: Ballantine Books.

Field, K. (2018, June 3). Freshmen 'Are souls that want to be awakened'. *The Chronicle of Higher Education*. Retrieved from https://www.chronicle.com/article/Freshmen-Are-Souls-That/243559

Florida International University. (2018). *Beyond possible 2020*. Retrieved from https://stratplan.fiu.edu

Freeman, S., Eddy, S. L., McDonough, M., Smith, M. K., Okoroafor, N., Jordt, H., & Wenderoth, M. P. (2014). Active learning increases student performance in science, engineering, and mathematics. *Proceedings of the National Academy of Sciences, 111*(23), 8410–8415.

Koch, A. K. (2017). Many thousands failed: A wakeup call to history educators. *Perspectives on History, 55*(5), 18–19.

Koch, A. K., & Foote, S. (2018). *Gateways to completion: Overview, evidence of strength, and summary of outcomes to date*. Brevard, NC: John N. Gardner Institute for Excellence in Undergraduate Education.

Koch, A. K., Prsytowsky, R., & Scinta, A. (2017). Maximizing gateway course improvement by making the whole greater than the sum of the parts. In A. Koch (Ed.), *Improving teaching, learning, equity, and success in gateway courses. New Directions for Higher Education* (180). San Francisco: Jossey-Bass.

Koch, A. K., & Rodier, R. (2014). *Gateways to completion guidebook*. Brevard, NC: John N. Gardner Institute for Excellence in Undergraduate Education.

LaGuardia Community College. (2018). *Academic requirements and policies*. Retrieved from https://www.laguardia.edu/uploadedFiles/Main_Site/Content/Academics/Catalog/PDFs/AcademicRequirementsAndPolicies.pdf

Mervis, J. (2011). Weed-out courses hamper diversity. *Science, 334*(6062), 1333.

National Academy of Sciences, National Academy of Engineering, and Institute of Medicine. (2011). *Expanding underrepresented minority participation: America's science and technology talent at the crossroads*. Washington, DC: The National Academies Press. Retrieved from https://doi.org/10.17226/12984.

Nevada State College. (2018). *Course assistant program*. Retrieved from http://nsc.smartcatalogiq.com/en/2017-2018/Catalog/Resources-Services-and-Referrals/Course-Assistant-Program

University of California at Berkeley. (2018). *Granting an incomplete grade*. Retrieved from https://registrar.berkeley.edu/faculty-staff/grading/incomplete-grades

University of Georgia Office of Student Financial Aid. (2018). *Grade changes and incomplete grades*. Retrieved from https://osfa.uga.edu/policies/enrollment-and-financial-aid/grade-changes-and-incomplete-i-grades/

University of Nevada, Las Vegas. (2018). *Transparency in learning and teaching in higher education*. Retrieved from https://www.unlv.edu/provost/teachingandlearning

U.S. Department of Education. (2018). *Staying eligible*. Retrieved from https://studentaid.ed.gov/sa/eligibility/staying-eligible

Washington and Lee University. (2018). *Academic regulations*. Retrieved from http://catalog.wlu.edu/content.php?catoid=3&navoid=219#Incomplete

Wilcox, E. W. (1911). The Weed. In *Poems of progress and new thought pastels by Ella Wheeler Wilcox* (p. 80). London: Gay & Hancock.

Yeager, D. S., & Walton, G. M. (2011). Social-psychological interventions in education: They're not magic. *Review of Educational Research, 81*(2), 267–301.

2

The Gateway Course Completion Line

The title of this chapter draws from W.E.B. Du Bois's 1903 book, *The Souls of Black Folk*, and its famous statement that "the problem of the Twentieth century is the problem of the color line." It may seem odd to readers that I chose to draw on Du Bois in a book about gateway courses. But I am doing so for good reason, with evidence to support my claim. Sadly, while the Jim Crow segregation of which Du Bois was writing is a part of the past, the color line still exists in some hidden but significant ways. As this chapter shows, race-based inequity manifests itself in gateway courses in some of the most significant ways seen in modern higher education. The methods and outcomes may be subtle. But they nevertheless carry serious societal ramifications, which I call the gateway course completion line.

To be clear, I agree with what Jeffery Selingo said in the *Washington Post* in 2018: "It is not that colleges should simply pass students through to graduation. But when only a little more than half of undergraduates make it to commencement, it cannot simply be the fault of students. At some point, colleges have to look inward at their own cultures and practices" (Selingo, 2018). When we look at the data, the call to look at cultures and practices—in this case, in gateway courses—becomes urgent.

The gateway course data I have been examining with my colleagues over the past six years show that while family income, first-generation status, and gender all correlate with poor performance in gateway courses, race and ethnicity seem to matter most. In this chapter, I provide some historical contextualization for that data—to help readers see that there is a connection between what is going on in gateway courses today and our nation's racial past. After that, I explore how unquestioned and seemingly timeless practices and policies used in gateway courses—methods that collectively I refer to as a "tyranny of practice"—favor more affluent and largely White students. I show how those practices and policies subtly but effectively cut out students of color from courses, cull them from programs of study, and ultimately deny them the dream of social mobility.

In short, this chapter shows that, when examined in-depth, few people experience greater hardship in gateway courses than students of color. Thus, in the twenty-first century, the gateway course completion line functions as a new form of color line. That line is subtler, without separate water fountains, lunch counters, or rest rooms. But it is equally as discriminatory and debilitating. The conclusion of this chapter shows this does not need to be the case. There are promising ways to make sure that quality is upheld and learning is deepened—ways that can end the tyranny of practice and erase the gateway course completion line.

The Gateway Course Completion Line Exposed

As you may have already inferred from my reference to the color line, in this chapter I have elected to focus extensively on outcomes for African American students in gateway courses. I could have concentrated on the outcomes of Native American students or Latinx students in gateway courses. My decision to focus on African American students to highlight and explain issues of race in gateway courses is not meant to marginalize or trivialize any other narratives. Simply stated, I chose to focus on African American students because the data compel me to do so.

In an article published in the May 2017 edition of *Perspectives on History*, I shared the findings from a study of grades and other outcomes in introductory U.S. history courses showing that failure rates were anywhere from 20% to more than 100% higher for students of color, first-generation students, and/or low-income students when compared to those of White, non-first-generation, and non-low-income backgrounds. I also shared how these higher rates of failure directly correlated with significantly greater rates of college departure, particularly for students who were otherwise in good academic standing. In other words, failing even one foundation-level course was correlated with leaving college even if the student was otherwise doing well academically (Koch, 2017). While the article focused on outcomes in introductory history courses, Brent Drake (the individual who did the statistical analysis used in the article) found the same trends in introductory college accounting, biology, chemistry, calculus, college algebra, English rhetoric and composition, and general psychology courses. In other words, this is a widespread issue across introductory "gateway" courses of many types, as the two tables that follow show. A bit of context on the data found in the two tables is merited. The data come from a study of DFWI rates in eight gateway courses published in early 2019 (Koch & Drake, 2019). Specifically, the study examined the DFWI rates in eight introductory courses—principles of accounting, general biology, general chemistry, English composition, introductory U.S. history, college algebra, Introductory college calculus, and general psychology—at thirty-six different colleges and universities in the United States (see Column A in both Tables 2.1 and 2.2). The thirty-six institutions include seven community colleges, two proprietary (for-profit) four-year institutions, eight independent (private) four-year institutions, and nineteen public four-year institutions—twenty-nine four-year and seven two-year institutions in total. The twenty-nine four-year institutions further break down into six baccalaureate colleges, fourteen masters colleges and universities, and nine doctoral universities. All thirty-six institutions provided data for the study, but not all thirty-six institutions provided data for all the courses examined. This is why the number of institutions with data considered for each course (see Column B in both Tables 2.1 and 2.2) varies between 31 and 34. Enrollments in the gateway course sections across the institutions in the study varied between slightly above

13,000 students in calculus to over 96,000 in introductory college writing/English composition (see Column C in both Tables 2.1 and 2.2).

Table 2.1 shows that race matters. And when focused on race, being African American seems to matter most consistently across the courses. In six of the courses—Principles of Accounting, General Biology, English Composition, History (U.S. Survey), Math—Algebra, and General Psychology—African Americans have the highest DFWI rate when compared to the other race-ethnicity groups shown in Table 2.1. In Math—Calculus, African American students' DFWI rate is only one-tenth of a percentage point (0.1) lower than that of Latino/Hispanic students who have the highest DFWI rate in the course—47.8% for African American students compared to 47.9% for Latino/Hispanic students. And in General Chemistry, only Native Americans have a higher DFWI rate than African Americans. Based on the research Drake and I did, the number of Native Americans in General Chemistry courses across the institutions—105 total students—is dwarfed by the African American enrollment in the course—2,039 students (Koch & Drake, 2019). That there are so few Native Americans enrolled in Chemistry across the institutions, and that they fail at such high rates, are tragedies that should not be overlooked. However, based on the sheer numbers, the slightly lower failure rates of African Americans in the course cannot be dismissed either.

Table 2.2 shows that first-generation status and family income—the latter defined as students receiving a Pell grant—also matter. First-generation students (Column D in Table 2.2) always have a higher DFWI rate than their non-first-generation counterparts (Column E in Table 2.2). And students receiving the Pell grant (Column F in Table 2.2) always have a higher DFWI rate than their non-Pell-grant counterparts (Column G in Table 2.2). But what is also worth noting is that DFWI rates for African American, Native American, and Latino/Hispanic students in the same courses are almost always higher than for first-generation and low-income (Pell) students (Table 2.1).

What is clear from these two tables is this—when it comes to who fails and who succeeds in gateway courses, race matters.

TABLE 2.1
Rates of D, F, W, and I Grades by Course and Selected Race/Ethnicity Designations

A. Course	B. Number of Institutions	C. No. of Students Across the Courses	C. Average DFWI Rate	D. African American DFWI Rate	E. Native American DFWI Rate	F. Latino/Hispanic DFWI Rate	G./Caucasian DFWI Rate
Principles of Accounting	32	17,538	30.2%	42.7%	36.9%	35.5%	25.9%
General Biology	33	24,636	29.8%	41.9%	37.4%	35.0%	25.9%
General Chemistry	31	20,987	29.4%	47.2%	54.5%	42.0%	26.3%
English Composition	34	96,258	22.8%	27.7%	25.0%	24.7%	19.7%
History (U.S. Survey)	32	27,666	25.1%	42.4%	40.5%	32.9%	21.4%
Math—Algebra	34	55,335	34.5%	49.9%	39.0%	30.6%	38.3%
Math—Calculus	32	13,253	34.3%	47.8%	32.3%	**47.9%**	31.5%
General Psychology	34	91,108	25.4%	40.2%	33.4%	28.6%	21.4%

TABLE 2.2
Rates of D, F, W, and I Grades for Gateway Courses by First-Generation and Pell Statuses

A. Course	B. Number of Institutions	C. No. of Students Across the Courses	C. Average DFWI Rate	D. First-Gen. DFWI Rate	E. Non-First-Gen. American DFWI Rate	F. Pell DFWI Rate	G. Non-Pell DFWI Rate
Principles of Accounting	32	17,538	30.2%	31.4%	30.3%	31.9%	27.3%
General Biology	33	24,636	29.8%	34.1%	29.0%	34.1%	28.8%
General Chemistry	31	20,987	29.4%	32.8%	26.9%	32.4%	28.3%
English Composition	34	96,258	22.8%	24.5%	21.3%	23.3%	20.2%
History (U.S. Survey)	32	27,666	25.1%	26.1%	22.4%	28.5%	22.7%
Math—Algebra	34	55,335	34.5%	38.7%	31.5%	38.0%	31.7%
Math—Calculus	32	13,253	34.3%	36.9%	33.4%	37.5%	29.9%
General Psychology	34	91,108	25.4%	28.2%	23.0%	28.9%	23.6%

Race seems to matter even more than family income and first-generation status. And when focused on race, being African American seems to matter most. Thus, it is clear that the color line lives on—recast, at least in one form, as the gateway course completion line. Few people are aware of the historical underpinnings and contemporary practices that contribute to this harsh reality.

The Tyranny of Practice—How the Gateway Course Completion Line Is Upheld

In the twenty-first century, small unquestioned practices frequently used in gateway courses often reinforce systematized inequity in ways completely unseen by those who use the practices. These classroom practices and the culture of which they are a part most deleteriously impact students who are historically least likely to enroll and subsequently succeed in higher education in the United States (National Academies of Sciences, Engineering, and Medicine, 2016; Seymour & Hewitt, 1997). Instructors using these common and unquestioned practices are unwittingly engaging in what I call a tyranny of practice. Through this tyranny of practice, instructors are unintentionally maintaining a systemically rooted inequitable status quo—one that most disadvantages students from poorer and/or non-White families.

A brief scan of accounts of U.S. history from even just the twentieth century would allow one to quickly compile of a list of policies and laws that have harmed persons of color and the poor in the United States: Practices such as immigration laws, "redlining," de jure and de facto forms of segregation, property tax-based school funding, voter suppression and redistricting efforts, and mandatory sentencing requirements have left poor and non-White students less likely to go to college and highly unlikely to complete a degree even if they do attend (Anderson, 2016; Thurston, 2017). Sadly, today, the greatest determinant of the probability of going to and completing a degree in college is family wealth. And wealth correlates directly with race in the

United States (Asante-Muhammad, Collins, Hoxie, & Nieves, 2017).

The effect of centuries of legalized inequity in the United States still shapes the preparation of the increased number of minority and low-income students who are coming to college in the twenty-first century. The students who are deleteriously impacted by this unequal preparatory experience are being met by practices in college classrooms that were never designed for them and that don't facilitate better learning and outcomes for them once they enroll. In short, collegiate teaching practices did not create systemic structural inequity in the modern United States, but they are doing little to mitigate it.

For example, the use of didactic teaching practices (a.k.a. lecture) prominent in introductory courses in many disciplines does not work particularly well with twenty-first-century learners—especially those from historically underrepresented and/or underserved backgrounds (Freeman et al., 2014; Murphy Paul, 2015). In their *New York Times* op-ed essay, "Are College Lectures Unfair," Annie Murphy Paul notes that students from poor and minority backgrounds are "disproportionately likely to have attended low-performing schools and to have missed out on the rich academic and extracurricular offerings familiar to their wealthier White classmates, thus arriving on campus with less background knowledge." This presents a serious problem, Murphy Paul continues, "since research has demonstrated that we learn new material by anchoring it to knowledge we already possess." She goes on to note that "(t)he same lecture, given by the same professor in the same lecture hall, is actually not the same for each student listening; students with more background knowledge will be better able to absorb and retain what they hear." Compounding issues in traditional lecture courses is the fact that minority, low-income, and first-generation students are often confronted by "a high-pressure atmosphere that may discourage them from volunteering to answer questions, or impair their performance if they are called on." Murphy Paul notes that this is highly problematic, because "(r)esearch in psychology has found that academic performance is enhanced by a sense of belonging—a feeling that students from these groups often acutely lack" (2015).

In addition to lecture, many forms of academic support used in conjunction with gateway courses favor the "haves" over the "have-nots." Research shows that tutoring and other forms of voluntary supplemental support, frequently offered as optional and outside of regular class time, carry with them deep stigma that frequently dissuade students who are already questioning whether or not they belong in college from taking part (Arendale, 2010a, 2010b). Voluntarily using academic support triggers what Steele, Aronson, and their research partners have dubbed "stereotype threat"—the fear of one's actions leading to the confirmation of negative stereotypes about a person's racial, ethnic, gender, or cultural group (Steele & Aronson, 1995; Steele, 1997, 1999; Spencer, Steele, & Quinn, 1999). The degree to which a student perceives that his or her help-seeking and/or other course-related actions reinforce a stereotype has been shown to directly correlate with negative effects on academic performance (Thoman, Smith, Brown, Chase, & Lee, 2013). This is true even at the nation's most selective institutions. For example, Robert and Thomson (1994) found, in their study of their students at the University of California Berkeley, that students of color believed that it would be "discrediting" to seek assistance, and many of them did not do so as a result.

Moving beyond race, providing academic support outside of class as an optional experience favors those who do not work full-time and/or who have the means to easily get to and from an office on campus. This is most acute when supplemental support is offered in traditional campus help centers that are open only for a limited number of hours and only during the regular work day. As the educational scholar Kay McClenney quipped, "At-risk students don't do optional" (McClenney, 2012)—to which I must add, they often do not "do optional" because they literally cannot find the time to do so.

In addition to lecture and optional, out-of-class academic support offerings, grading practices also have negative implications for historically underrepresented and underserved students in gateway courses. And when it comes to grading in gateway courses, one of the prime engines of inequality is grading on a curve.

It is not hard to see why people find the idea of grading on a curve so appealing. The approach, at least theoretically, subscribes to the belief that through effort students can move beyond their humble origins in life. Work hard and you get rewarded with a position on the right hand of the curve—the passing part. Don't work hard, and you wind up on the left hand, failing side. Advocates for the curve approach also point out the flaws in other methods of grading. Awarding grades, the argument goes, is always unfair in some respect because of the subjective nature of grading. In keeping with this argument, the use of a curve is believed to be the fairest of approaches since the normal distribution—the statistical distribution method behind curve grading, which is also known as "the bell curve"—removes individual subjectivity from the act of grading. Seen in this manner, curve grading is viewed as a formulaic vehicle for fairness, not an arbitrary mechanism for favoritism.

However, when taking a deeper look, grading on a curve may very well be just another arbitrary judgment mechanism masked by a formula. It transfers the immediate responsibility for judgments about grades from an instructor or a group of instructors to a mechanism—a decision done by a distribution. Alas, curve grading models tend to push students from the least privileged of backgrounds to the low-performing end of the scale and, in turn, wind up pushing many of them out of the system altogether. In other words, students from under-resourced high schools and families without a college-going tradition will disproportionately constitute those who fall on the left-hand side of a normal distribution (Darling-Hammond, 1998; Grant, 2016). With this reality exposed, merit-based systems such as grading on a curve often are, in fact, what Jo Littler in *The Guardian* labeled, "a smokescreen for inequality" (Littler, 2017).

Chris Hayes reinforces this point in his book *Twilight of the Elites*. Hayes notes, among many examples provided, how systems created to reward merit are actually being gamed by the privileged, who use them to generate a self-perpetuating elite. In other words, those who already have intellectual and financial capital, pass that along to their friends and family. Those who lack it, cannot do so—which means children from affluent and more educated backgrounds will invariably do better in "merit-based" systems than their counterparts from equally talented but less resourced backgrounds (Hayes, 2012).

Take, for example, admission to prestigious colleges and universities—specifically one of the main tests used to quantify student merit—the SAT. The SAT "began as a high-minded reform. Applicants would be chosen for intellectual prowess and compete for their spot on a level playing field." However, due to access to better resourced schools and the means to pay for test preparation, "the rich get lots of time to practice on it, while even smart poor kids don't" (Friedersdorf, 2012).

As I mentioned earlier, historically in the United States there has been a correlation between race and wealth—with Whites having and gaining more wealth when compared to other races, especially African Americans. According to the Census Bureau's Current Population Survey, Black families in America earn $57.30 for every $100 in income earned by White families today. Over time, this means Black families accumulate less wealth. This is supported by the sobering Census Bureau Population Survey statistic that shows for every $100 in wealth held by White families, Black families hold just $5.04 (Badger, 2017). In other words, White families are, on average, nearly twenty times—1,984.1%—wealthier than their African American counterparts.

With the documented evidence shared above about that historical relationship between race and income in the United States, and the connection between income and academic performance, readers should not be surprised by the fact that in 2018, African Americans had the lowest combined SAT composite score average of all race/ethnicity groups. The combined score for Blacks on the math and evidence-based reading and writing sections of the SAT was 946. This compares to an overall average score of 1060 and an average score for White test takers of 1,123 (Jaschik, 2018). The "merit-based" college entrance examination seems to actually be "inherit-based"—rewarding those who come from means.

The "merit-based" grading on a curve approach takes over where the SAT merit-based scoring process leaves off. While theoretically "race- or need-blind," the advantages possessed by more affluent and disproportionately White students, and the basic zero-sum constructs associated with curve grading, mean that minority students, particularly Blacks, have to fail. By its very nature, curve grading pits students in competition with each other. If, as standard distribution models often mandate, one-third of the students have to earn less than a C, and family wealth and race are the best predictors for who does or does not succeed in the courses, then it is little surprise that so few students of color make it to the next course in the curricular sequence. As one frustrated biology professor who taught junior- (third-year) level courses at a research university on the East coast once told me, "I keep hearing about the need to have more students of color earning degrees in biology. I teach a 300-level course. And I have to tell you, by the time the students make it to my course, there are *no* students of color left anymore. What am *I* supposed to do about this issue?"

This situation has led some educators at colleges and universities to begin to reject the curve grading approach as well as other age-old but all-too-often unquestioned policies and practices used in gateway courses—the policies and practices I have combined under the heading "The Tyranny of Practice." Emphasizing mastery of content over competition-based filtering, cutting-edge educators are going through a kind of conversion process. David Laude, senior vice provost for enrollment and graduation management and a professor of chemistry at The University of Texas at Austin—one of the nation's most prestigious public research universities—is one such convert. In fact, his conversion has led him to become a kind of lay "preacher" whose "sermons" focus on the rejection of old methods in courses in favor of new grading, teaching, and learning practices.

In an op-ed that appeared in both the *Texas Tribune* and the *Fort Worth Star Telegram* Laude's assertions mirror those I shared earlier in this chapter. He notes, "Rich students usually graduate from college. Poor students usually don't." "(T)he underlying reason why many students don't graduate" according to Laude is "the grading curve" which he describes as "the venerable measure that instructors use to separate the best students from the worst" (Laude, 2014).

In a manner similar to that which I used earlier in this chapter, he goes on to share that if you "(e)nd up too far to the left on the bell curve too often . . . your chances of graduating fall sharply. And historically, that has applied disproportionately to the disadvantaged." Laude then laments that the grading curve just reinforces the "idea of education as competition in which instructors select for the best and in some cases forget the rest." He notes how this model "often hurts students, especially freshmen, who are finding their footing" (Laude, 2014).

Pointing to new innovations in teaching and classroom-based technologies that he is employing in his 500-student chemistry course, Laude shares that there is a need to shift from the "merit-based" traditional approach—in the process casting away practices like curve grading and the lecture-only methodology—to a "mastery-based" model. Such a model recognizes and rewards student growth over time, provides students with opportunities to learn from mistakes within a course, and, in the process, facilitates deeper learning (Dweck). Admitting that there are skeptics who see what he is doing as the diminishment of standards, Laude shares, "I can assure you my course material has only gotten more challenging through the years, and more importantly, far more learning is going on now than before." He concludes:

> In the coming years, I imagine that the most successful teaching models will effectively blend the very best of what technology has to offer with the value that only comes with face-to-face learning. What should disappear in the process is the grading curve. New strategies will be needed for ranking our students and guiding them toward professional schools and into the workforce, but there will also be a lot more educated talent to spread around—and Texas will be much the better for it.
> (Laude, 2014).

While Laude focused his closing comments in his op-ed on Texas, they have considerably broader implications. In fact, the implications are national. While not using the phrases, and focusing on income rather than race, Laude is, in fact, describing the issues associated with the gateway course completion line and the tyranny of practice that upholds it. He describes how high failure rates for disadvantaged students in his course compelled him to use less lecture in favor of more active learning strategies, how these strategies help embed experiences and forms of support—some available via technology—within the course as opposed to outside of it, and how he stopped grading on a curve in favor of allowing hard-working students from all backgrounds to show that they have progressively mastered the content. In short, he chose to stop being a participant in the maintenance of the status quo by no longer adhering to the tyranny of practice.

The Way Forward and Why It Has to Happen

I don't know a single instructor of college courses who, when presented with this reality—especially when supported with evidence from his or her own courses—has called for upholding this tyranny of practice. On the contrary, like Laude, they are moved to look for alternatives and take action. Alas, few postsecondary institutions encourage their faculty to examine and redesign their introductory courses with a lens toward addressing historic and systemic inequity. Even fewer support their faculty in efforts to do so (National Academies of Sciences, Engineering, and Medicine, 2016, pp. 86–87). And, for at least two main reasons, this must change.

First, colleges and universities in the United States are experiencing one of the greatest demographic shifts they have ever encountered. Declining birth rates starting in the early twenty-first century and continuing at least until 2036 mean that there are simply fewer traditional aged students who will be coming to college (Bransberger & Michelau, 2016). The demographic makeup of this smaller traditional-aged college-going population is also undergoing a massive shift. By 2045, the United States will become a "majority-minority" nation (Frey, 2018). But for children under the age of eighteen, that tipping point has already been realized (Yoshinaga, 2016). In other words, the majority of the college-going student body soon will be constituted by the very same students who historically do not fare well in introductory college courses. Failure to recognize and take active steps to address the needs of this shifting demographic will mean that institutions will lose even more public trust—as a result of not serving the students they enroll well—and resources—since declining enrollments will lead to even less state support and/or tuition revenue.

But there is a second and more compelling reason why what is done in gateway courses must change. It comes down to living up to our institutions' core values and mission statements. We cannot tell students and families that we help promote social mobility and advance justice if, in fact, we maintain a gateway course completion line that limits possibilities for all but an already well prepared and more affluent select few. This is where faculty come in.

I must strongly assert that I am by no means blaming faculty for the systemic inequity described in this or any of the other chapters in this book. But I am openly *naming* them as a primary agent for change in the contemporary postsecondary reform movement—change that directly addresses structural racism and classism. I am also not calling for a reduction of standards in the courses that these faculty teach. In fact, I am calling for the exact opposite—an increase in expectations for our learners and for those who teach them, with strong support and incentivization for the faculty reform agents. Faculty of all types—full-time, part-time, tenured, adjunct—should be supported and rewarded for this work. They should be introduced to transparent and inclusive pedagogies—teaching methods such as those used by Bryan Dewsbury that many faculty never learned about in graduate school (Dewsbury, 2018). And they should be helped to intentionally work with others at their institutions to continuously improve teaching, learning, and student success in the courses they teach. In a chapter in a recent book on the first college year, John Gardner and I note how, unfortunately, faculty have been largely left out of the contemporary postsecondary student success movement—often through no choice of their own (Koch & Gardner, 2017). This has been detrimental to us all—especially to our students. This sin of omission has led to the promotion of the tyranny of practice.

But faculty and higher education administrators—particularly those who teach or provide support of any kind for gateway courses—can help change this. Doing so will be hard work. But it is very important work. In fact, as educators, it may be the most important work we undertake in our careers. And it starts with changing small things that have big student failure consequences, thereby putting an end to the tyranny of practice in the classroom and the gateway course completion line that the tyranny of practice enforces.

The Gateway Course Completion Line—A Contemporary Manifestation of the Color Line

Of course, the color line and the gateway course completion line are not the same thing. They are, however, closely linked. In fact, the gateway course completion line is one of many contemporary forms of the color line—a next-generation separating and segregating engine.

The gateway course completion line is a more furtive form of the color line. Its sinister nature is masked by the broader popular notion and widely circulated narrative that significantly greater numbers of low-income and historically underrepresented students now have access to college. The fact that many of these very same students are "weeded out" through a tyranny of practice—sometimes merely weeks after being included in an institutional press release touting the "record diversity" of the incoming class—is not understood as contradictory in many colleges or universities. The common refrain is that the students who did not succeed in gateway course lack motivation. They lack the proper preparation. They are not the "better students" the institution once had or should have. They probably belonged elsewhere. Just not at this institution. Or lunch counter. Or water fountain.

Du Bois made frequent use of the phrase "the color line" in his essays and addresses throughout the latter nineteenth and twentieth centuries. But he may not have been the originator of the phrase. Frederick Douglas authored an article in the *North American Review* using the expression as the title over twenty years before Du Bois published *The Souls of Black Folk* (1881, pp. 567–77). While the origins of the phrase may be cloudy, its meaning as a reference to post-abolition race-based segregation in the United States is clear. Du Bois summarized the effects of the color line succinctly when he noted that the central question associated with it was "how far differences of race . . . will hereafter be made the basis of denying to over half the world the right of sharing to their utmost ability the opportunities and privileges of modern civilization" (1900, p. 125).

Du Bois gradually expanded his concept of the color line to include not just race but also socioeconomic class and other distinctions. For example, after visiting the ruins of the Warsaw ghetto following World War II, Du Bois wrote how "the problem of . . . caste in the United States was no longer . . . a separate and unique thing as I had so long conceived it. It was not even solely a matter of color and physical and racial characteristics" (1952, p. 14).

Fast forward to the present, and we find that the blatantly codified segregation of the Jim Crow era is gone. But the forms of race and class-based inequity and stratification that Du Bois noted throughout his life remain. They are reinforced by educational experiences that have not changed to reflect the shifting demographic nor the changing economic and workforce dynamics. And this necessitates a Du Bois-like central question for us to consider. How much longer are we willing to allow differences of race and socioeconomic status—and the benefits of accrual and privilege associated with those demographics—to serve as the major basis of denying many of the nation's undergraduates the right of sharing the opportunities and privileges of the modern global economy and society? Because, as the evidence and narrative found in this chapter suggest, that is, in essence what happens for a large number of students who enroll in and don't succeed in gateway courses.

This is why the problem of twenty-first-century higher education is the gateway course completion line. It is a problem that can be addressed, if colleges and universities are willing to look at their cultures, policies, and practices with an eye toward scaling approaches that advance equitable, high-quality learning outcomes—strategies that help more low-income, first-generation, and historically underrepresented students cross the finish line. Now that we have established the challenge before us, the remainder of this book will be devoted to offering a way forward, to erase the gateway course completion line and make gateway courses truly the gateways to student success.

References

Anderson, C. (2016). *White rage: The unspoken truth of our racial divide*. New York: Bloomsbury.

Arendale, D. R. (2010a). Access at the crossroads: Learning assistance in higher education. *ASHE Higher Education Report, 35*(6), 23–54.

Arendale, D. R. (2010b). Current challenges and controversies for learning assistance. *ASHE Higher Education Report, 35*(6), 7–22.

Asante-Muhammad, D., Collins, C., Hoxie, J., & Nieves, E. (2017). *The road to zero wealth: How the racial wealth divide is hollowing out America's middle class*. Washington, DC: The Institute for Policy Studies.

Badger, E. (2017, September 18). Whites have huge wealth edge over Blacks (but don't know it). *The New York Times*. Retrieved from https://www.nytimes.com/interactive/2017/09/18/upshot/black-white-wealth-gap-perceptions.html

Bransberger, P., & Michelau, D. (2016). *Knocking at the college door: Projections of high school graduates* (9th ed.). Boulder, CO: Western Interstate Commission for Higher Education.

Darling-Hammond, L. (1998). Unequal opportunity: Race and education. *The Brookings Review; Washington, 16*(2), 28–32.

Dewsbury, B. (2018, January 23). The soul of my pedagogy. *Scientific American*. Retrieved from https://blogs.scientificamerican.com/voices/the-soul-of-my-pedagogy/

Douglass, F. (1881, June). *The North American Review, 132*(295), 567–577.

Du Bois, W. E. B. (1900). Address to the Nations of the World. First Pan African Conference, London. Retrieved from http://www.blackpast.org/1900-w-e-b-du-bois-nations-world

Du Bois, W. E. B. (1903). *The souls of Black folk: Essays and sketches.* Chicago, IL: A. C. McClurg.

Du Bois, W. E. B. (1952). The Negro and the Warsaw Ghetto. *Jewish Life, 6*(7), 14–15.

Freeman, S., Eddy, S. L., McDonough, M., Smith, M. K., Okoroafor, N., Jordt, H., & Wenderoth, M. P. (2014). Active learning increases student performance in science, engineering, and mathematics. *Proceedings of the National Academy of Sciences, 111*(23), 8410–8415.

Frey, W. (2018). *The U.S. will become 'Minority White' in 2045, Census projects.* Brookings Institute. Retrieved from https://www.brookings.edu/blog/the-avenue/2018/03/14/the-us-will-become-minority-white-in-2045-census-projects/

Friedersdorf, C. (2012, June 14). The cult of smartness: How meritocracy is failing America. *The Atlantic.* Retrieved from https://www.theatlantic.com/politics/archive/2012/06/the-cult-of-smartness-how-meritocracy-is-failing-america/258492/

Grant, A. (2016, September 10). Why we should stop grading students on a curve. *The New York Times.* Retrieved from https://www.nytimes.com/2016/09/11/opinion/sunday/why-we-should-stop-grading-students-on-a-curve.html

Hayes, C. (2012). *Twilight of the elites: America after meritocracy.* New York: Crown Publishers.

Jaschik, S. (October 29, 2018). SAT scores are up, especially for Asians. *Inside Higher Ed.* Retrieved from https://www.insidehighered.com/admissions/article/2018/10/29/sat-scores-are-gaps-remain-significant-among-racial-and-ethnic-groups

Koch, A. K. (2017). Many thousands failed: A wakeup call to history educators. In *Perspectives on history* (pp. 18–19). Washington, DC: American Historical Association.

Koch, A. K., & Drake, B. M. (2019). *Digging into the disciplines II: Failure in historical context – The impact of introductory U.S. history courses on student success and equitable outcomes.* Brevard, NC: John N. Gardner Institute for Excellence in Undergraduate Education.

Koch, A. K., & Gardner, J. N. (2017). Transforming the 'Real First-Year Experience': The case for and approaches to improving gateway courses. In R. Feldman (Ed.), *The first year of college: Research, theory, and practice on improving the student experience and increasing retention*. New York: Cambridge University Press.

Laude, D. (2014, June 25). College grading curve is an antique. *Star-Telegram*. Retrieved from https://www.star-telegram.com/opinion/article3863119.html

Littler, J. (2017, March 20). Meritocracy: The great delusion that ingrains inequality. *The Guardian*. Retrieved from https://www.theguardian.com/commentisfree/2017/mar/20/meritocracy-inequality-theresa-may-donald-trump

McClenney, K. (2012). *A matter of degrees: Promising practices for community college student success (A first look). Center for community college student engagement*. Austin, TX: The University of Texas at Austin.

Murphy Paul, A. (2015, September 15). Are college lectures unfair? *New York Times Sunday Review*, p. 12.

National Academies of Sciences, Engineering, and Medicine. (2016). Barriers and opportunities for 2-year and 4-year STEM degrees: Systemic change to support diverse student pathways. In S. Malcom & M. Feder (Eds.), *Committee on barriers and opportunities in completing 2-year and 4-year STEM degrees. Board on science education, division of behavioral and social sciences and education. Board on higher education and the workforce, policy and global affairs*. Washington, DC: The National Academies Press.

Robert, E. R., & Thomson, G. (1994). Learning assistance and the success of underrepresented students at Berkeley. *Journal of Developmental Education, 17*(3), 4–6, 8, 10, 12, 14.

Selingo, J. J. (2018, June 8). Why do so many students drop out of college? And what can be done about it? *Washington Post*. Retrieved from https://www.washingtonpost.com/news/grade-point/wp/2018/06/08/why-do-so-many-students-drop-out-of-college-and-what-can-be-done-about-it/?utm_term=.5dadddd2db81

Seymour, E., & Hewitt, N. (1997). *Talking about leaving: Why undergraduates leave the sciences*. Boulder, CO: Westview Press.

Spencer, S. J., Steele, C. M., & Quinn, D. M. (1999). Stereotype threat and women's math performance. *Journal of Experimental Social Psychology, 35,* 4–28.

Steele, C. M. (1997). A threat in the air: How stereotypes shape the intellectual identities and performance of women and African-Americans. *American Psychologist, 52,* 613–629.

Steele, C. M. (1999). Thin ice: "Stereotype threat" and black college students. *The Atlantic Monthly, 284*(2), 44–47, 50–54.

Steele, C. M., & Aronson, J. (1995). Stereotype threat and the intellectual test performance of African-Americans. *Journal of Personality and Social Psychology, 69,* 797–811.

Thoman, D. B., Smith, J. L., Brown, E. R., Chase, J., & Lee, J. Y. K. (2013). Beyond performance: A motivational experiences model of stereotype threat. *Educational Psychology Review, 25*(2), 211–243.

Thurston, C. (2017). *At the boundaries of home ownership: Credit, discrimination, and the American state.* New York: Cambridge University Press.

Yoshinaga, K. (2016). Babies of color are now the majority census says. *NPR.org.* Retrieved from https://www.npr.org/sections/ed/2016/07/01/484325664/babies-of-color-are-now-the-majority-census-says

3

On Belonging—The Case for Learning Mindsets, Metacognition, and Faculty as Teaching and Learning Experts

This chapter explores the importance of belonging and associated psychological approaches to learning. The "who belongs" versus the "who does not belong"—which all too often directly correlates with the "haves" versus the "have-nots." It is also about what can be done to build a sense of belonging and a culture of human growth through what goes on in college classrooms—that is, if you care about having postsecondary education institutions live up to the promises of human growth and social mobility that are often published in their mission statements and admissions materials.

The Current Context—From the "Amateur in the Operating Room" to the Teaching and Learning Expert

The historian David Pace in his essay, "The Amateur in the Operating Room: History and the Scholarship of Teaching and Learning" (2004) makes the argument for applying what Ernest

Boyer (1990) first dubbed "the scholarship of teaching and learning" to actual practice in the classroom span well beyond the field of history. Pace (2004) asserts:

> The very existence of a growing body of scholarship on teaching and learning is making it increasingly difficult to deny that many aspects of our practice as college history teachers can be grounded in such knowledge. It now seems quite possible that we can replace an understanding of teaching based on folk traditions and unfounded personal impressions with one rooted in a rigorous and collective examination of what fosters student learning. Under such circumstances, it would seem to be a violation of the most basic ethical commitments of our profession to accept as normal what Salvatori and Donahue have called "willed ignorance and the arrogance of not-knowing." Pride in ignorance should be no more honored in teaching than it is in other aspects of our professional life.
>
> (p. 1191)

According to Pace, we should no more trust an untrained teacher in the classroom—even if they are content gurus—than we should trust doctors to conduct surgery if they were never trained in operating room procedures—even if they "aced" all of their anatomy and physiology courses. Content-rich faculty cannot be the equivalent of medical knowledge-rich amateurs in the operating room. The fact that we have allowed this situation in postsecondary education teaching is an artifact of a bygone era. As Pace quipped during a workshop at the 2016 annual meeting of the American Historical Association, "In the 1970s and 1980s, the classroom was like the bathroom. You knew something important happened there; and you *never* talked about it!" (Koch, 2017, p. 12).

But in the twenty-first century, we *should* talk about the classroom. And we must undertake widespread action to improve what is occurring there. Furthermore, we can apply the body of knowledge available to instructors now that did not exist twenty or more years ago and make sure that it is being applied effectively.

It is irresponsible for institutions of higher learning not to help their faculty learn about and apply that knowledge. In fact, failure to systematically support and reward efforts to apply evidence-based teaching and learning practices is more than irresponsible. It borders on the malfeasant—especially when one considers the twenty-first-century student demographic discussed in the previous chapters of this book.

In the twenty-first century, responsible educators have no excuses for not advocating for and supporting wide-scale efforts to transform teaching, learning, and the structures and practices associated with college courses. Academic leaders must guarantee that the high level of content mastery that instructors possess is matched by an equally high level of teaching and learning expertise. In short, postsecondary leaders of all types must make sure that those who teach their courses are not the classroom equivalent of book-smart-but-experience-lacking surgeons. They must make sure that their discipline experts are also experts in the most effective ways to teach and foster deep learning in the field in which they are offering instruction.

Belonging Matters—The Theoretical Case for Fostering Belonging in Gateway Courses

It is beyond the scope of this chapter to comprehensively enumerate and deeply illustrate the rich array of strategies that fit under the broader heading of "evidence-based teaching and learning practices." However, based on what I personally experienced and, more importantly, what is known about the millions of students who constitute the contemporary postsecondary student body, it is well within the scope of this chapter to focus on evidence-based teaching and learning practices that address the psychological need to belong—practices that foster a more supportive learning environment for students who largely have been made to feel like *persona non-grata* in college classrooms.

As explained by the psychologist Marianna Pogosyan, "Much of human behavior, thought, and emotion stems from our psychological need to belong . . . other people matter. In fact, they matter so much, that they become a source of our self-esteem." She continues, noting that as humans we "may even base our self-concepts not only on our unique traits and characteristics (individual self), but also on the attachments we form with significant others (relational self), and the social groups we identify with (collective self), thus, continuously navigating our self-definitions between 'I' and 'we'" (2017, para. 1).

The emotional consequences of belonging have been studied extensively. Pogosyan notes, "Bonds with other people can become causes for happiness. Supportive social networks can act as buffers against stress. The feeling of being connected to others can be a protective factor against depression" (2017, para. 2). Students are one of the major groups in which the effects of belonging have been studied at length. A student's sense of belonging with peers and teachers positively affects academic performance and motivation (Schlossberg, 1989). A lack or decrease in perceived belonging can lead to poor academic performance and, ultimately, departure from a program of study or even postsecondary education altogether.

One particular negative affect associated with belonging—or more precisely, a lack of belonging—is what Claude Steele and Joshua Aronson dubbed "stereotype threat" (1995). Essentially, stereotype threat is the "risk of confirming, as self-characteristic, a negative stereotype of one's group" (Steele & Aronson, 1995, p. 797). In their definitive study of stereotype threat—the study in which they coined the phrase—Steele and Aronson (1995) documented their experiments that showed that African American college students performed worse than their White peers on the same standardized tests when the African American students were reminded before taking the tests that their racial group tends to do poorly on such exams. When their race was not emphasized, however, African American students performed similarly to their White peers. Steele, Aronson, and their colleagues showed comparable findings in their subsequent scholarship (cf. Steele, 1997; Steele, 1998; Steele, James, &

Barnett, 2002; Steele, Spencer, & Aronson, 2002). Other scholars have found stereotype threat applicable to many additional demographic groups—such as women in male-dominant fields such as math (Walsh, Hickey, & Duffy, 1999; Ambady, Shih, Kim, & Pittinsky, 2001) students from low-income families when juxtaposed with their higher-income counterparts (Harrison, Stevens, Monty, & Coakley, 2006), and Whites compared to Asian males in math (Aronson Lustina, Good, Keough, Steele, & Brown, 1999). In short, in situations, such as in classrooms, where a stereotype is applicable, "one is at risk of confirming it as a characterization, both to one's self and others who know the stereotype." When "the stereotype involved demeans something as important as intellectual ability, the threat can be disruptive enough . . . to impair intellectual performance" (Steele & Aronson, 1995, p. 808).

An additional belonging-related issue is the dynamic that Clance and her colleagues first came to call "the imposter phenomenon"—commonly referred to today as "imposter syndrome" (Clance, 1985; Clance & Imes, 1978; Clance & O'Toole, 1987; Langford & Clance, 1993). Imposter syndrome is defined as the "psychological experience of believing that one's accomplishments came about not through genuine ability, but as a result of having been lucky, having worked harder than others, or having manipulated other people's impressions" (Langford & Clance, 1993, p. 495). In academics, imposter syndrome frequently manifests itself as some students view their success in courses and academic programs of study as somehow being fraudulent, even if they have no legitimate reason to do so. Research shows that women—particularly women of color—are susceptible to imposter syndrome in academic environments (Attewell & Domina, 2011; Miller & Kastberg, 1995). While men do question whether they belong in academic environments, being a woman and/or a person of color makes a person prone to some of the most extreme forms of struggle and doubt in the United States—especially in the classroom (Walton & Cohen, 2007). These experiences of racism and sexism increase the probability that women and students of color may experience impostor phenomenon and, as a result, question whether they truly belong in an academic institution and/or program of study.

While there is undoubtedly bad and highly discomforting news in the scholarship about stereotype threat, imposter syndrome, and the broader belonging construct, the fact that these are psychological in nature is cause for optimism. The outcomes have to do with the interaction between persons in college settings—disproportionately students of color, women, and students from low-income families and/or first-generation backgrounds—and their environments. In short, the context of the learning environment influences group identity and self-perception. This, then, is the silver lining in the bad news about belonging. Rather than being the result of race and gender, belonging issues are psychological products of the environment—an environment that can and must be changed to meet the needs of the rapidly changing college student demographic. As Grawe (2018) argues in his book *Demographics and the Demand for Higher Education*, demographics need not be destiny. But they will be if educators do nothing to change the way that foundational educational experiences—particularly gateway courses—convey messages to students about who does or does not belong in college today.

Belonging and Beyond—Learning Mindsets and Metacognition as Means to a More Just End

Given the importance of belonging, contemporary efforts focused on improving teaching and learning in college classrooms are often focused on the use of approaches that communicate to students that they are respected, valued by their instructors and peers, and that they fit into the learning environment both culturally and socially. These kinds of approaches are often grouped together under the heading of "learning mindset" strategies. The Mindset Scholars Network, a group of more than forty scholars from nearly twenty-five postsecondary institutions, is a group of researchers dedicated to the scientific understanding of students' beliefs about learning and school in order to improve student outcomes and expand educational opportunity. Members of the Network argue that learning mindsets play a role in students' persistence and achievement in college (2015). The Network places particular emphasis on researching strategies that advance three forms of learning mindsets: growth mindset, sense of belonging, and purpose and relevance.

Growth mindset is often credited to the work done by Carol Dweck and her colleagues at Stanford University. According to Dweck, a "*growth mindset* is based on the belief that your basic qualities are things you can cultivate through your efforts. Although people may differ in every which way—in their initial talents and aptitudes, interests, or temperaments," she continues, "everyone can change and grow through application and experience" (2006, p. 7). This contrasts with *a fixed mindset*, which Dweck defines as the belief that one's "qualities are carved in stone" (2006, p. 6). In other words, a growth mindset conveys the belief that intelligence can be developed. A fixed mindset conveys that intelligence and attitudes are set at birth.

While growth and fixed mindsets shape how students view themselves and what they like to do—take, for example, students who do not do well in math and have come to believe from an early age that they are "not good at math"—mindsets are not simply the result of how students view themselves. In fact, they are often the result of how instructors and educational institutions have subtly, often unknowingly, but nevertheless effectively conveyed messages about aptitude to students through course registration and classroom practices.

In their article "The Role of Ethnicity in Choosing and Leaving Science in Highly Selective Institutions," Elliott, Strenta, Adair, Matier, and Scott share how beliefs prevalent in gateway courses across colleges and universities lead to consistent levels of failure regardless of institutional admissions selectivity (1996). Elliott, Strenta, Adair, Matier, and Scott note how students at Harvard University had, by and large, the same science degree completion rates as students at all the other colleges and universities included in their study. Specifically, science degree completion rates were directly correlated with standardized test (SAT) score ranges. Students in the bottom third of the SAT range at all the institutions included in the study had a science completion rate that was essentially three to four times lower than students in the top third. One would think that getting into Harvard or other competitive schools would increase the likelihood that a student would complete a degree in a particular field of choice—in this case, science. After all, Harvard takes only the highest achieving students. But this assumption proved to be incorrect—at least in the study Elliott, Strenta, Adair, Matier, and Scott published. Regardless of how high the institution's SAT average was, the science degree completion trend held true across every institution considered. This suggests that there is more at play than student aptitude and work ethic. Those who teach in the field of science may very well have the expectation that a certain subset of students have to fail—because that is their accepted norm. The prevailing attitude seems to be: "Two-thirds of the students have always failed, so they always must." As Shirley Malcom and her colleagues document conclusively in their recent book *Barriers and Opportunities for 2-Year and 4-Year STEM Degrees*, this has to do with a fixed ability mindset culture among those who teach. They note:

> The culture that students encounter when studying STEM has an effect on their interest, self-concept, sense of connectedness, and persistence in STEM. Many students encounter messages that their success in STEM fields requires natural ability in math or science or very early exposures to high-quality training, which tends to be associated with lower persistence among women and minorities.
>
> (Malcom & Feder, 2016, p. 73)

The fixed mindset culture of which Malcom and Feder write limits possibilities for many students. Disproportionately, those who get "weeded" out come from minoritized and low-income family backgrounds (Westin, Seymour, Koch, & Drake, 2019). And make no mistake, this is not simply a dynamic in STEM courses and associated programs of study (Koch & Drake, 2018, 2019).

The alternative to applying fixed mindsets in courses and programs of study can be found in work occurring at the University of Texas at Austin (UT Austin). One of the premier research universities in the United States that is confronted with a shifting demographic where low-income and historically minoritized students account for a growing portion of the undergraduate enrollment, UT Austin has been a leader in the application of growth mindset to its courses and the undergraduate experience at large. This is, in large part, the result of the leadership of a chemistry professor turned administrator, David Laude (Tough, 2014), mentioned in the previous chapter. During a 2012 conference address in which Laude was explaining why he changed his approach to courses and has worked to do the same with the undergraduate experience broadly, he shared:

> You know, I've been teaching freshman chemistry for 20 years now. That's 20,000 students. People always thought I was a pretty good teacher, but every year I wouldn't pass about 20 percent of my students. There are 4,000 kids whose hopes and dreams I destroyed, and I just want to say I'm sorry.
>
> (Seale, 2019, para. 1)

Working with David Yeager, a UT Austin professor of psychology, and others, Laude fostered an environment of growth inside his chemistry course as well as in other programs he helped the University launch. Laude does this because he finds little fulfillment in helping students who have had life-long advantages be the only ones who succeed in his courses. He notes, "When you have that, then you walk into my class and get the high grade on my test, all I've done is perpetuate what has always been true." The real challenge and satisfaction, according to Laude, comes from helping students from rural or inner-city backgrounds "overcome 18 years of *not* being advantaged so that they can succeed. Because if they don't, if I decide to not pass them in that freshman year, you can write off them ever going to medical school," Laude adds, "then the economic divide just gets worse and worse in the state of Texas" (Seale, 2019, para. 9, emphasis in original).

One of the noted growth mindset efforts Laude undertook is the redesign of his introductory chemistry course. On the first day of class, he tells students they can all earn an A. Over the term, he gives them many classroom-based opportunities to work hard to do so—cultivating learning skills and enthusiasm along the way. The changes have resulted in dramatic improvement in his students' performance. Now, most of the students in Laude's course earn the A grade he tells them they can achieve. This is not because he has "watered down" the course—students in Laude's course section take the same final as students in all other chemistry sections. Rather, according to *New York Times* contributing writer David Kirp, the result is because Laude "smartened up as a teacher. He became their coach, not their judge" (2019, para. 15). In other words, as opposed to believing that one quarter to one half of all students had to fail, he told his students that they all can succeed, and he made it his personal mission to use his course to show them how.

An extension of growth mindset, sense of belonging is the second learning mindset that the Mindset Scholars Network deems significant, especially for students from historically disadvantaged and disenfranchised groups. Students who possess a sense of belonging in school "feel socially connected, supported, and respected. They trust their teachers and their peers" and they also "feel a sense of fit at school. They are not worried about being treated as a stereotype and are confident that they are seen as a person of value" (Mindset Scholars Network, 2015). Belonging goes well beyond the classroom. It can be cultivated or undermined by things as simple as routine communications institutions send to their students on payments or policies (Brady, Cohen, & Walton, 2017). But the classroom is a place where it must be conveyed—for doing otherwise can make even the best structured out-of-class experiences come across as window dressing and, worse yet, empty promises.

The rationale for why instructors must develop a sense of belonging in their courses has already been discussed in this chapter. What follows are a few examples of how belonging can be fostered in classrooms.

One belonging strategy frequently promoted in faculty development workshops is one of the simplest. To help students feel like they belong, get to know and use their names. Better yet, get to know and use their preferred names *and* their chosen pronouns.

But belonging is about more than just knowing that your instructor knows who you are—even if that is a good start. Belonging is about seeing oneself in the context in which one is studying—for example, having case studies in an STEM course of the work of Katherine Coleman Johnson, an African American female mathematician who calculated flight trajectories for Project Mercury and other missions, or Mary Golda Ross, a member of the Cherokee nation who, as the first known Native American female engineer, made significant contributions to aerospace design used in space travel.

Belonging can also be reinforced, or shaken, through the way institutions shape and enforce academic policies. Researchers examining students' experiences of being placed on academic probation—an experience that can quickly evoke feelings of shame and stigma leading students to disengage from the academic environment—find that some simple modifications to the messaging about the probationary status can drastically change student reenrollment behaviors (Brady et al., 2017). As summarized by Romero (2018, p. 4), revising academic probation letters so that they "clearly signal the institution's ongoing respect for and valuing of the student, acknowledge the real challenges students may face, and emphasize probation as a process and the potential to return to good academic standing has been found to reduce students' feelings of shame and stigma" and increase "the likelihood that students took advantage of academic supports available on campus." In one study, the revised probation letter was correlated with a near doubling of the rate at which students returned to good academic standing—going from 26% to 43% (Yeager, Purdie-Vaughns, Hooper, & Cohen, 2017).

Purpose and relevance is the third approach emphasized by the Learning Mindset Scholars Network. Strategies that convey purpose and relevance help students "value their schoolwork because it gets them to believe it is relevant to their lives and/or will help them connect to a purpose that is bigger than themselves—whether it is a contribution to their family, their community, society at large, or something else" (Mindset Scholars Network, 2015). One of my favorite purpose and relevance approaches is called Ethnographies of Work (EoW), a strategy created and employed by Mary Gatta, Niesha Ziemke, and other faculty and staff at the City University of New York Stella and Charles Guttman Community College (Guttman Community College, 2019).

Guttman College is the City University of New York's newest campus. All of its students are commuters, and primarily come from low-income, first-generation, and historically minoritized populations (Gatta & Hoffman, 2018). A model for embedding purpose and relevance in multiple courses during the first college year, EoW helps student use ethnographic strategies to pose questions about workplaces, occupations, and career paths. In their EoW courses, students learn about the myths and stereotypes about work, determine the types of work that matter to them, explore that ever-changing nature of work in a fast-paced global economy, and begin to make connections between themselves and work they might do in their future careers (Guttman Community College, 2019). This is done through learning about and applying ethnographic and historical tools. For example, early in their first EoW course, students read an excerpt of Marx's *Das Kapital* specifically focusing on worker alienation (1992). They use that reading as the basis for a class discussion on Marx's stages of alienation in industrial workplaces and follow that with an activity in which they reflect on if and/or how alienation can apply to today's service economy workers. They then go out to various service-sector workplaces—such as local franchises of chain coffee shops or bakeries—and observe workers and the labor process. They take pictures and field notes and then write a paper applying what they learned about alienation to service work (M. Gatta, personal communication, October 1, 2019). As explained by Howard Wach, Guttman College's vice president for academic affairs in 2019, the EoW model helps students blend "critique with career"—allowing them to reflect on what they thought work was, what they want it to be, and how they can be agents in making relevant educational choices that lead them to these broader desired career options and associated social mobility (H. Wach, personal communication, January 25, 2019).

Purpose and relevance strategies need not be as intensive as the EoW model. For example, education researchers used a simple activity in which two sets of students in a science course were randomly assigned journal assignments. Over the span of a semester, the experimental group was asked to periodically reflect on the usefulness of the course material in their own lives. Students in the control group were asked just to summarize the material that was covered in the course. All students were asked about their expectations to do well in the course at the beginning of the term. Students in the experiment group who initially expressed having low expectations for success in the course—students who saw the least value of the course to their lives—earned higher grades in the course than their counterparts in the control group. The outcomes suggest that even simple, periodic, purpose and relevance activities undertaken in conjunction with a course can make big differences (Hulleman & Harackiewicz, 2009).

Collectively, the three learning mindsets described in this chapter—growth mindset, purpose and relevance, and sense of belonging—have been shown to positively address psychological factors that, if left unaddressed, can inhibit student success—particularly the success of students from low-income, first-generation, and historically minoritized backgrounds. Mindset strategies clearly are powerful. However, they can only do so much. In my experience, learning mindset approaches can and should be supplemented by strategies that help students think about and, as a result, more intentionally approach, the act of learning itself—approaches that broadly fit under the heading of "metacognition."

While the broader concept of metacognition can be traced back to Aristotle, the way the term is being used and defined in contemporary teaching and learning discussions and in this book must be attributed to John H. Flavell's contribution to the 1976 book *The Nature of Intelligence* edited by L. B. Resnick. In his chapter "Metacognitive Aspects of Problem Solving," Flavell defines metacognition as "one's knowledge concerning one's own cognitive processes and products or anything related to them, e.g. the learning-relative properties of information or data" (Flavell, 1976, p. 232). In simple form, metacognition is thinking about one's own thinking.

Metacognition is increasingly being used to help students reflect on how they learn, and how they can succeed in college. One of the most widely recognized contemporary experts on embedding metacognitive "learning skills" in college courses is Saundra Yancy McGuire, retired assistant vice chancellor and professor of chemistry at Louisiana State University. Drawing on work spanning more than forty years—eleven of which were spent at Cornell University as the director of that institution's Center for Learning and Teaching—McGuire published the well-received 2015 book, *Teach Students How to Learn*. In that book, and its 2018 companion, *Teach Yourself How to Learn* (McGuire, 2018), McGuire provides strategies that both faculty and students can use to improve learning skills and, as a result, learning and motivation in college courses. While it is outside of the scope of this chapter to summarize the lessons she conveys in those books, it is important to convey why she is sharing these strategies.

In her plenary address at the 2017 Gateway Course Experience Conference, a meeting sponsored by the Gardner Institute, McGuire noted how over her more than forty years of work in colleges and universities, her teaching colleagues often lamented about their students' lack of motivation. They would complain about how students would stop showing up and simply not care about the work, and these complaints seemed to be increasing as the student body was diversifying. McGuire continued,

> In my experience, there are lazy and unmotivated students. I would estimate that somewhere between 10–15% of all students in courses truly lack the motivation or maturity to do the work we are asking them to do. But that does not explain why many of our courses have 30, 40, 50 percent, and even higher rates of D, F, W, and I grades.
>
> (McGuire, 2017)

In other words, those "lazy and unmotivated" students are often anything but lazy or unmotivated. There are psychological (learning mindset) and metacognitive (learning skills) barriers keeping them from succeeding.

Like learning mindsets, metacognitive learning skills need to be taught and reinforced. As responsible educators, we cannot expect twenty-first-century learners to know how to learn, to possess the social and cultural capital generally associated with wealth and privilege. We can expect them to be responsible for their learning if we are willing to teach them how to do so. What McGuire and others are showing is that this is possible at scale if educators care enough and are supported enough by their institutions to learn how to teach today's students. As the concluding section of this chapter will show, there are important social implications for all of this work—implications that get directly at the value, relevance, and very soul of higher education in the twenty-first-century United States.

Summary and "So What?"—Why Learning Mindsets and Metacognition Matter, and How They Help Move Classrooms From Being Tools of Social Reproduction to Sites for Social Mobility

Sadly, one need not strain their imagination too hard to see the toll that lack of belonging and an environment that does not cultivate learning mindsets can take. Recent research conducted in educational settings makes the case that a sense of belonging is associated with motivation, success, and persistence (Freeman, Anderman, & Jensen, 2007; Hausmann, Schofield, & Woods, 2007; Hoffman, Richmond, Morrow, & Salomone, 2002–2003). Alas, that same growing body of scholarship tells us that developing a sense of belonging can be particularly challenging for students from minoritized groups (Hurtado & Carter, 1997; Schlossberg, 1989; Stephens, Fryberg, Markus, & Johnson, 2012; Strayhorn, 2012).

What often happens in classrooms acts to perpetuate and exacerbate the issues associated with not belonging. Faculty should not be blamed for many of the actions that were historically repeated in their courses. Far too often, faculty simply were never shown other possibilities. As proffered by David Pace (2004), they functioned, quite unknowingly, as "amateurs in the operating room." But in the contemporary era, we know better. We have options to do otherwise. And we are morally obligated to do so.

This chapter highlighted learning mindset and metacognitive strategies that, in my experience and based on the scholarly evidence I shared, constitute some of the most important pedagogical "options" that contemporary faculty can and should apply in their courses. The learning mindsets include: (1) strategies that foster a growth, as opposed to a deficit mindset; (2) approaches that create and maintain students' sense of belonging; and (3) practices that help students develop purpose and perceive the relevance of what they are learning in their courses. The metacognitive strategies I described help students learn how to learn. In other words, they teach students how to master course content through what actually happens in the course itself.

In the first and second chapters of this book I described in some detail the nation's changing demographic and how this change is leading to both a shrinking traditional-aged college student population as well as a steadily diversifying student body. Therefore, higher education institutions as we know them must change the way they teach their students, especially in gateway courses. Failure to do so will mean that even greater proportions of students will be forced out of the academy and that the bulk of those leavers will come from historically minoritized backgrounds and/or low-income families. And this is why learning mindsets and metacognitive strategies matter. Simply stated, faculty need to learn about and apply these strategies because failure to do otherwise will result in a betrayal of the public and the communities that colleges and universities were established to serve.

It is my firm belief that learning mindsets and metacognitive strategies are some of the most important approaches faculty can use in their gateway courses to avoid becoming—or remaining—agents of social reproduction. My deep concern about college and universities—especially their faculty—being unknowing agents of social reproduction is the reason why I have included a chapter on learning mindsets and related metacognitive strategies in this book.

Social reproduction is the theoretical construct that explains how, in modern capitalist economies, workers are "produced." Most readers are aware how, in the modern economy, workers produce commodities. But workers themselves have to be produced—and this "production" is more than just about being born. It requires social processes and systems that yield the forms of labor—skilled and unskilled—necessary for the economy (Bhattacharya, 2017).

If, like me, you believe that education should be an endeavor that levels the playing field—a means for helping poor students and students from historically oppressed groups break generational cycles of poverty and subordination—then what is going on in gateway courses at many institutions should be deeply troubling. If you truly examine who succeeds in gateway courses at colleges and universities in the United States today, it will become readily apparent that those who do well in courses disproportionately come from backgrounds where they had prior access to better elementary and secondary schooling, better extracurricular opportunities, and better computers and books. Thus, unknowingly, but nevertheless quite effectively, gateway courses are one of the main postsecondary education structures that reproduce these societal patterns. While social reproduction clearly does not only occur in the college classroom, gateway courses are one of the largest vehicles for reinforcing or repudiating the concentration of wealth and privilege in the academy. Further, while faculty cannot be blamed for centuries of structural barriers that predate their careers and even their birth, they must be named as the primary agents for change in light of the significance of the courses they teach.

Learning mindset and metacognitive strategies are powerful tools faculty can use to reinforce their students' sense of worth and gradually erase years of classroom-based alienation. They are strategies that help faculty to, in turn, help their students mitigate the gaps associated with privilege and prior education—so that the promises we make about postsecondary education being a vehicle for social mobility are actually fulfilled for all students—especially those who do not "look like one of us."

So, the next time you hear a colleague lament, "I wish admissions got us better students," ask them if they are using any of the strategies described in this chapter. If they have never heard of them, let alone employed them on a consistent basis, maybe what the institution actually needs are teachers and environments that foster and reward the development of America's new majority. Anything else simply replicates an unjust system, to the detriment of the learners, the institutions, and, ultimately, the communities and nation of which we are all a part.

References

Ambady, N., Shih, M., Kim, A., & Pittinsky, T. L. (2001). Stereotype susceptibility in children: Effects of identity activation on quantitative performance. *Psychological Science, 12*, 385–390. doi: 10.1111/1467-9280.00371

Aronson, J., Lustina, M., Good, C., Keough, K., Steele, C., & Brown, J. (1999). When white men can't do math: Necessary and sufficient factors in stereotype threat. *Journal of Experimental Social Psychology, 35*, 29–46. doi: 10.1006/jesp.1998.1371

Attewell, P., & Domina, T. (2011). Educational imposters and fake degrees. *Research in Social Stratification and Mobility, 29*(1), 57–69. doi: 10.1016/j.rssm.2010.12.004

Bhattacharya, T. (2017). How not to skip class: Social reproduction of labor and the global working class. In T. Bhattacharya (Ed.), *Social reproduction theory: Remapping class, recentering oppression* (pp. 68–93). London: Pluto Press.

Boyer, E. L. (1990). *Scholarship reconsidered: Priorities of the professoriate.* Princeton, NJ: Carnegie Foundation for the Advancement of Teaching.

Brady, S. T., Cohen, G. L., & Walton, G. M. (2017). Revising the Scarlet Letter of Probation: Reframing Institutional Communications Reduce Shame and Stigma and Enhance Student Success. Paper Presented at the American Educational Research Association Annual Meeting, San Antonio, TX.

Clance, P. R. (1985). *The impostor phenomenon: Overcoming the fear that haunts your success.* Atlanta, GA: Peachtree.

Clance, P. R., & Imes, S. A. (1978). The impostor phenomenon in high achieving women: Dynamics and therapeutic intervention. *Psychotherapy: Theory, Research, and Practice, 15,* 241–247. doi: 10.1037/h0086006

Clance, P. R., & O'Toole, M. A. (1987). The impostor phenomenon: An internal barrier to empowerment and achievement. *Women in Therapy, 6,* 51–64. doi: 10.1300/J015V06N03_05

Dweck, C. S. (2006). *Mindset: The new psychology of success.* New York: Random House.

Elliott, R., Strenta, A. C., Adair, R., Matier, M., & Scott, J. (1996). The role of ethnicity in choosing and leaving science in highly selective institutions. *Research in Higher Education, 37*(6), 681–709.

Flavell, J. H. (1976). Metacognitive aspects of problem solving. In L. B. Resnick (Ed.), *The nature of intelligence* (pp. 231–236). Hillsdale, NJ: Erlbaum.

Freeman, T. M., Anderman, L. H., & Jensen, J. M. (2007). Sense of belonging in college freshmen at the classroom and campus levels. *The Journal of Experiential Education, 75*(3), 203–220. doi: 10.3200/JEXE.75.3.203-220

Gatta, M., & Hoffman, D. (2018). *Putting vocation at the center of the curriculum: The student experience in CUNY's ethnographies of work course.* Washington, DC: Stella and Charles Guttman Community College, CUNY: The City University of New York, and Jobs for the Future. Retrieved from https://www.jff.org/resources/vocation-center-curriculum/

Grawe, N. D. (2018). *Demographics and the demand for higher education.* Baltimore, MD: Johns Hopkins University Press.

Guttman Community College. (2019). *Ethnographies of work.* Retrieved from https://guttman.cuny.edu/academics/academic-programs/first-year-experience/ethnographies-of-work/

Harrison, L. A., Stevens, C. M., Monty, A. N., & Coakley, C. A. (2006). The consequences of stereotype threat on the academic performance of white and non-white lower income college students. *Social Psychology of Education: An International Journal, 9*(3), 341–357. doi: 10.1007/s11218-005-5456-6

Hausmann, L. R. M., Schofield, J. W., & Woods, R. L. (2007). Sense of belonging as a predictor of intentions to persist among African American and white first-year college students. *Review of Higher Education*, *48*(7), 803–839. doi: 10.1007/s11162-007-9052-9

Hoffman, M., Richmond, J., Morrow, J., & Salomone, K. (2002–2003). Investigating "sense of belonging" in first-year college students. *Journal of College Student Retention: Research, Theory & Practice*, *4*(3), 227–256. doi: 10.2190/DRYC-CXQ9-JQ8V-HT4V

Hulleman, C. S., & Harackiewicz, J. M. (2009). Promoting interest and performance in high school science classes. *Science*, *326*, 1410–1412. doi: 10.1126/science.1177067

Hurtado, S., & Carter, D. F. (1997). Effects of college transition and perceptions of the campus racial climate on Latino college students' sense of belonging. *Sociology of Education*, *70*(4), 324–345. doi: 10.2307/2673270

Kirp, D. (2019, August 23). What professors can do to boost student success [Blog post]. Retrieved from https://blog.oup.com/2019/08/what-professors-can-do-to-boost-student-success/

Koch, A. K. (2017). It's about gateway courses: Defining and contextualizing the issue. In A. K. Koch (Ed.), *Improving teaching, learning, equity, and success in gateway courses* (New Directions for Higher Education, No. 180, pp. 11–17). San Francisco, CA: Jossey-Bass.

Koch, A. K., & Drake, B. M. (2018). *Digging into the disciplines I: Accounting for failure—The impact of principles of accounting courses on student success and equitable outcomes*. Brevard, NC: John N. Gardner Institute for Excellence in Undergraduate Education. Retrieved from https://static1.squarespace.com/static/59b0c486d2b857fc86d09aee/t/5d94e2e7c9fa320443b775f2/1570038505729/Digging+Into+the+Disciplines+Accounting+for+Failure+022619.pdf

Koch, A. K., & Drake, B. M. (2019). *Digging into the disciplines II: Failure in historical context—The impact of introductory U.S. history courses on student success and equitable outcomes*. Brevard, NC: John N. Gardner Institute for Excellence in Undergraduate Education. Retrieved from https://static1.squarespace.com/static/59b0c486d2b857fc86d09aee/t/5d94e29b66b7f068b73e78ed/1570038428965/Failure+in+Historical+Context+-+The+Impact+of+Introductory+U.S.+History+Courses.pdf

Langford, J., & Clance, P. R. (1993). The imposter phenomenon: Recent research findings regarding dynamics, personality and family patters and their implications for treatment. *Psychotherapy, 30*(3), 495–501. doi: 10.1037/0033-3204.30.3.495

Malcom, S., & Feder, M. (Eds.). (2016). *Barriers and opportunities for 2-year and 4-year STEM degrees: Systemic change to support students' diverse pathways*. Washington, DC: The National Academies Press. doi: 10.17226/21739

Marx, K. (1992). *Capital: Volume 1: A critique of political economy* (B. Fowkes, Trans.). London, England: Penguin Classics. (Original work published 1867).

McGuire, S. Y. (2015). *Teach students how to learn: Strategies you can incorporate into any course to improve student metacognition, study skills, and motivation*. Sterling, VA: Stylus Publishing.

McGuire, S. Y. (2017, February 26). Teach Students How to Learn: Metacognition is the Key to Improving Success in Gateway Courses! Keynote Address Delivered at the 2017 Gateway Course Experience Conference, Las Vegas, NV.

McGuire, S. Y. (2018). *Teach yourself how to learn: Strategies you can use to ace any course at any level*. Sterling, VA: Stylus Publishing.

Miller, D. G., & Kastberg, S. M. (1995). Of blue collars and ivory towers: Women from blue-collar backgrounds in higher education. *Roeper Review, 18*(1), 27–33. doi: 10.1080/02783199509553693

Mindset Scholars Network. (2015). *Learning mindsets*. Retrieved from https://mindsetscholarsnetwork.org/learning-mindsets/

Pace, D. (2004). The amateur in the operating room: History and the scholarship of teaching and learning. *The American Historical Review, 109*(4), 1171–1192. doi: 10.1086/ahr/109.4.1171

Pogosyan, M. (2017). On belonging: What is behind our psychological need to belong? [Blog post]. Retrieved from https://www.psychologytoday.com/us/blog/between-cultures/201704/belonging

Romero, C. (2018). *What we know about belonging from scientific research*. Retrieved from http://mindsetscholarsnetwork.org/wp-content/uploads/2018/11/What-We-Know-About-Belonging.pdf

Schlossberg, N. K. (1989). Marginality and mattering: Key issues in building community. In D. C. Roberts (Ed.), *Designing campus activities to foster a sense of community* (New Directions for Student Services, No. 48, pp. 5–15), San Francisco, CA: Jossey-Bass.

Seale, A. (2019, September 19). *No left side of the curve*. Retrieved from https://news.utexas.edu/2019/09/19/no-left-side-of-the-curve/

Steele, C. M. (1997). A threat in the air: How stereotypes shape intellectual identity and performance. *American Psychologist, 52*(6), 613–629. doi:10.1037/0003-066X.52.6.613

Steele, C. M. (1998). Stereotyping and its threat are real. *American Psychologist, 53*(6), 680–681. doi: 10.1037/0003-066X.53.6.680

Steele, C. M., & Aronson, J. (1995). Stereotype threat and the intellectual test performance of African Americans. *Journal of Personality and Social Psychology, 69*(5), 797–811. doi: 10.1037/0022-3514.69.5.797

Steele, C. M., Spencer, S. J., & Aronson, J. (2002). Contending with group image: The psychology of stereotype and social identity threat. *Advances in Experimental Social Psychology, 34,* 379–440. doi: 10.1016/S0065-2601(02)80009-0

Steele, J., James, J. B., & Barnett, R. C. (2002). Learning in a man's world: Examining the perceptions of undergraduate women in male-dominated academic areas. *Psychology of Women Quarterly, 26,* 46–50. doi: 10.1111/1471-6402.00042

Stephens, N. M., Fryberg, S. A., Markus, H. R., Johnson, C. S., & Covarrubias, R. (2012). Unseen disadvantage: How American universities' focus on independence undermines the academic performance of first-generation college students. *Journal of Personality and Social Psychology, 102*(6), 1178–1197. doi: 10.1037/a0027143

Strayhorn, T. L. (2012). *College students' sense of belonging: A key to educational success for all students.* New York: Routledge.

Tough, P. (2014, May 15). Who gets to graduate? *The New York Times Magazine.* Retrieved from https://www.nytimes.com/2014/05/18/magazine/who-gets-to-graduate.html

Walsh, M., Hickey, C., & Duffy, J. (1999). Influence of item content and stereotype situation on gender differences in mathematical problem solving. *Sex Roles: A Journal of Research, 41*(3–4), 219–240. doi: 10.1023/A:1018854212358

Walton, G. M., & Cohen, G. L. (2007). A question of belonging: Race, social fit, and achievement. *Journal of Personality and Social Psychology, 92*(1), 82–96. doi: 10.1037/0022-3514.92.1.82

Westin, T. J., Seymour, E., Koch, A. K., & Drake, B. M. (2019). Weed-out classes and their consequences. In E. Seymour & A.-B. Hunter (Eds.), *Talking about leaving revisited: Persistence, relocation, and loss in undergraduate STEM education* (pp. 207–259). New York: Springer Publishing Company.

Yeager, D. S., Purdie-Vaughns, V., Hooper, S. Y., & Cohen, G. L. (2017). Loss of institutional trust among racial and ethnic minority adolescents: A consequence of procedural injustice and a cause of life-span outcomes. *Child Development, 88*, 658–676. doi: 10.1111/cdev.12835

4

Weeding Out the Weed-Out Culture

I am writing this chapter—and this book—because well-intentioned educators are often guilty of perpetuating myths that prop up a weed-out culture. It is a culture in which we academics were groomed for the positions we now hold. It is a culture that is upheld by words like "rigor," "standards," "tradition," and "grade inflation." Too often, it is a culture that does not get questioned, for doing so requires academics to question the very system that produced us. And it is a culture that is an artifact of an era when privileged students—chiefly affluent, male, and White—went to college to further maintain their privilege and the hegemony on which that privilege was founded.

This chapter addresses the "weed-out culture" that is alive, well, and seemingly self-replicating in and around gateway courses and the programs of study of which those courses are a part. It is the latter aspect—the self-replicating nature of the weed-out culture—that concerns me the most. That culture is propagated by generations of academics who were groomed in and rewarded by the Darwinian "survival of the fittest" ethos. As a result, at best, some if not most academics seem unaware about the weed-out culture's existence and their role in it. At worst, even if they are aware of that culture, too many educators are unwilling or feel unable to change it.

I hadn't planned to write this chapter. It just kind of happened one Labor Day weekend. What I had initially planned to do that weekend was have a quiet break from the endless back-to-back Zoom meetings and incessant stream of emails that had come to constitute my life in 2020. I had intended to do a bit of reading—to catch up on back issues of journals and magazines. I began by reading an online edition of the *Chronicle of Higher Education*. And that is when my Labor Day weekend plans changed. After reading Frederik deBoer's essay "Some Students Are Smarter Than Others (and That's OK)" from the August 27, 2020 edition of the *Chronicle of Higher Education* (deBoer, 2020), I was compelled to write what has become this chapter.

I do not hold deBoer solely responsible for the arguments he made in his essay. Instead, I view his essay as a representative sample of the broader arguments that support the "weeding out" of students. As the following pages will show, changing the weed-out culture starts with acknowledging that as academics we have great privilege, and that privilege may be leading us to reproduce the inequitable structures, practices, and inequitable culture that produced us. We also have the power and research at our disposal to do better.

The Perpetuation of Academic Myths

In accordance with deBoer's view of the higher education landscape, "not all students possess the underlying ability necessary to flourish in some fields." What's more, student ability cannot be dramatically improved—it is "fixed" at birth. If educators would just acknowledge this, they could better go about performing what deBoer describes as "a necessary but unfortunate function" of screening out students. Reflecting on a conversation with a fellow graduate student during his time at Purdue, deBoer recounted how he came to be aware that "only one in three students who started as an engineering major would finish with the degree, and that early courses in the major were actually designed to be 'weed out' classes, meant to compel students to drop the major and choose another." In a matter-of-fact manner, deBoer writes, "It was far better for them to do so early, before they had accumulated a lot of credits." Getting them to drop early was, in fact, according to deBoer, "an act of mercy."

As straightforward as the logic seems, it is equally, if not more, so flawed. In fact, the argument is based on misinformation. While the anecdote about only one-third of students succeeding in engineering at Purdue is presented as such—an anecdote— it is shared as a model to emulate—an aspirational system for maintaining standards and rigor. The fact is the outcomes shared in the anecdote are patently incorrect. According to data publicly available at the time deBoer wrote his essay, 68.7% of students who started in engineering at Purdue graduated with an engineering degree six years later. In the decade prior to 2013, the six-year graduation rate for engineers at Purdue never dipped below 50.8%; and in the period spanning 2009 through 2020 it was always above 61.0% (Purdue University Data Digest, 2020).

Make no mistake, my response has very little to do with graduation rates from engineering at Purdue. It has to do with the misperceptions that inversely correlated graduation rates should somehow serve as an indicator of quality, the belief that contemporary graduation rates are much lower than they actually are, the thought that rates should be kept low to maintain standards, and that student abilities are set in stone. Yes, there was an era when accomplished academic leaders would stand at the front of an auditorium during orientation and proudly state to the new student audience, "Look to your left, then look to your right, two of the three of you will not be seated in these seats at graduation." But that metric has long since ceased to be a measure of quality across higher education in the United States. For good reason.

The Historical Origins of the Unjust Weed-Out Culture

You can't talk about failing or succeeding in weed-out courses without considering grades. It turns out that the grading system largely used in education today is not as old as we might think. While exit exams existed at Harvard as early as 1646, grades for work done in college were first employed by Yale in 1785 when the institution began designating graduating seniors with one of four marks: *Optimi,* second *Optimi, Inferiores,* and *Perjores* (Smallwood, 1935). Around the same time, Yale started using the same system for giving all students credit for performance in individual classes, but the marks were hidden from the students themselves and not reported externally (Bagg, 1871). During the early to mid-nineteenth century, other institutions, such as Harvard, William and Mary, and the University of Michigan, began experimenting with grading policies of their own (Schinske & Tanner, 2014) even if most of the institutions at the time kept no formal record of the grades (Schneider & Hutt, 2014).

In the late nineteenth century, as colleges and universities grew in both number and size, coordination between these institutions became necessary in a variety of areas, including the meaning of grades. In 1884, Mount Holyoke began grading students with A, B, C, D, and E grades. Each grade was correlated with a percentage range, with E grades being given for student performance lower than 75%. In 1888, Mount Holyoke replaced the E grade with an F—so that the lowest grade was more readily associated with failure (F) as opposed to excellence (E). In 1890, Harvard adopted the same grading approach, and over the course of the late nineteenth and early twentieth centuries other institutions followed suit. Despite this, the A to F grading approach that seems so ubiquitous to educators today did not take hold on a large-scale basis until the 1940s (Schinske & Tanner, 2014).

Thus, it took nearly 300 years for the grading system to develop from its origins as graduation exams at Harvard to the system we know today. That "system" is barely eighty years old. We would be remiss if we did not consider this history, and the broader context in which this grading system developed.

Grades must be understood as an artifact of an era when, as D-L Stewart wrote in the June 2020 edition of *Change,* "A student would be a 'gentleman' scholar" (Stewart, 2020). As Stewart notes, the gentleman scholar idea, like the very foundation of higher education in the United States itself, draws from a model for higher education started in England at the turn of the second millennium and further developed, in what would become the United States, by elite and affluent property owners. This model yielded a higher education system "restricted by design to the children of the landed gentry"—nearly all of whom were White males who came from economically propertied families at a time when "property" could be defined as enslaved persons.

According to Stewart, gentlemen scholars were prepared for life after graduation by "being schooled in morality and knowledge of the world's wisdom." Producing gentlemen scholars "required a campus that was cloistered from the life of the common world with an inaccessible and detached curriculum." This philosophy, Stewart continues, "was never intended to be inclusive of a diversity of people or equitable and just outcomes. Only certain people could fulfill the ideal of 'gentlemen scholars.'" Stewart (2020) then tells us:

> This continues today with the oft-repeated refrain that not everybody needs to go to college, restating the belief that college is only for certain privileged people like higher education's first students almost four centuries ago. When everybody does not need to be in college, then whether everybody has an equitable college experience becomes a moot issue.

Stewart's emphasis on an equitable college experience cannot be understated. He is correct to point out the racial and income dynamics associated with who gains access to and succeeds in higher education today. Stewart makes it clear that the postsecondary education was not designed for the students it serves now and will serve in the years to come. At the time of my writing of this chapter, some states have made it nearly impossible to speak about, let alone act on, the inequitable outcomes in higher education. As Nathan Grawe (2018, 2021) makes clear in his research, states ignore demographics at the peril of their students and the communities of which they are a part.

To be clear, when I write about equity and justice, I am writing about equity and justice for all students. Again, *all* students. This includes, but is by no means limited to, White students from low-income families who, as Martin Luther King Jr. pointed out in 1967, outnumbered African Americans living in poverty at a rate of 2-to-1 (King, 2010). Today that gap is even higher (Shrider, 2023).

In short, we cannot have a meaningful conversation about improving the college experience if we cannot examine who does or does not succeed in gateway courses and how the policies and practices of the past may not help the nation in the present or the future. Equitable attainment means equity for all. One must be able to study and design for that like the future of our democracy and its citizens depends on it. Because it does.

This brings me back to deBoer and his essay—the article that compelled me to write about weed-out culture in this book. His essay does not even use the terms equity or justice or consider that some students come into privilege at birth while others lack the opportunities associated with family wealth and stature. By emphasizing what deBoer calls "individual cognitive differences," the essay fails to acknowledge that inequitable outcomes associated with family demographics and income exist and stubbornly persist in academe. These differences are historic and structural in nature. In my research and experience, nowhere is this more prevalent than in the "weed out classes" that deBoer views as a necessity for the maintenance of higher education's standards.

My assertions are supported by an essay I wrote for the May 2017 edition of the American Historical Association's *Perspectives on History*. Based on an analysis of course success rates at over thirty-six colleges and universities in the United States, this article summarized the findings of a quantitative analysis done with my colleague Brent Drake. The essay and the research that undergirded it make it clear that gateway courses, as they have existed at many colleges and universities for decades, perpetuate systemic inequality found in society and, in the process, reinforce established social hierarchies (Koch, 2017). As supported by other studies that Brent Drake and I have written and published since the 2017 *History Perspectives* essay, inequitable outcomes in gateway courses are not just an issue in the discipline of history

(Koch & Drake, 2018, 2019). Those unjust results span all disciplines with one persistent finding—students of color, students from low-income families, and students who are the first in their families to go to college are the students most likely not to succeed in foundation-level courses.

To make matters worse, as Cliff Adelman's quantitative analyses of massive postsecondary datasets have shown, when students do not succeed in gateway courses, they don't just leave the institutions at which they earned the non-passing grades, they leave college altogether (Adelman, 1999, 2006). In other words, contrary to popular belief, students who get "weeded out" of gateway courses, especially if they are students of color or receive need-based federal grants, often tend not to find another major in which they can be more successful.

But if success in weed-out classes was, in fact, an indicator of intellectual merit, then high-ability students should persist in and complete the degree programs that these courses feed. Here again, evidence does not support that argument. As Tim Weston, Elaine Seymour, Brent Drake, and others (including me) make clear in *Talking About Leaving Revisited*, women, students from the lowest socioeconomic backgrounds (Pell grant recipients), and students from first-generation backgrounds often perform well, if not better than their counterparts, in foundational-level courses. It merits pointing out that there is considerable overlap with family income and race/ethnicity in the United States—meaning that a large portion of the students of color who attend come from lower socioeconomic backgrounds. But even when students from these backgrounds are "high performers" in the gateway courses they take, they leave the STEM disciplines at higher rates than their counterparts—especially compared to their underperforming male counterparts from more affluent families. In other words, "weed-out" courses are not culling out only the lowest performers. Rather, they function as structures that primarily privilege family income as well as gender and race (Westin, Seymour, Koch, & Drake, 2020).

I have worked with thousands of faculty members over more than thirty years of my career to date. I have yet to meet one who, when confronted with this evidence, feels that the status quo should be maintained. My faculty colleagues care deeply about their students and the lives they will lead. But few faculty are provided this evidence. Even fewer are supported by their institutions to make changes over the long-term once they do see the results. Overwhelmingly, college faculty are content experts. They largely have not been nurtured to be teachers and instructional designers. They are products of what has been come to be called the "fixed intellect" school of thought. In the next section, I share some successful ways to support faculty as they move from the history of fixed intellect thinking to a growth mindset orientation.

Antidotes for the Toxic Weed-Out Culture

The idea that intellect is, in some way, fixed at birth inherent in deBoer's essay flies in the face of a steadily growing body of evidence that has come from the field of psychology over the past fifteen to twenty years. Stemming from the work of Carol Dweck and her colleagues at Stanford University, and with the help of entities such as the Student Experience Research Network (2023), postsecondary educators from across the higher education landscape are conducting research and applying evidence-based practices that communicate to students that they are respected, they belong, that they are valued by their instructors and peers, and that they fit into the learning environment both culturally and socially. These kinds of approaches are often grouped together under the heading of "learning mindsets." A summary of research published by the Mindset Scholar Network—the precursor of the Student Experience Research Network—reports that changes in these learning mindsets "can alter students' academic behaviors in ways that can lead to sustained improvements in performance" (Quay & Romero, 2020). In other words, knowledge and intellect are not as fixed as those who subscribe to the notion of the gentleman scholar would have us believe—and there is evidence to back this.

It was the awareness that fixed thinking led to inequitable outcomes that prompted David Laude, whom you will remember from previous chapters is a professor of chemistry at the University of Texas (UT) at Austin, to work with David Yeager, a UT Austin professor of psychology and member of the Mindset Scholars Network, to foster an environment of growth in an array of academic initiatives at UT. Laude did this because, according to an interview published by his university, he found little fulfillment in helping students who have had lifelong advantages be the only ones who succeed in his courses. He noted, "When you have that, then you walk into my class and get the high grade on my test, all I've done is perpetuate what has always been true." The real challenge and satisfaction, according to Laude, come from helping students from rural or inner-city backgrounds "overcome 18 years of not being advantaged so that they can succeed. Because if they don't, if I decide to not pass them in that freshman year, you can write off them ever going to medical school," Laude added, "then the economic divide just gets worse and worse in the state of Texas" (Seale, 2019).

Fortunately, Laude is not alone in his pursuits. With support from the Andrew W. Mellon Foundation, and in conjunction with the Gardner Institute—the organization that employs me—the American Historical Association launched History Gateways (American Historical Association, 2019). That effort helped history faculty at eleven colleges and universities across the United States use evidence-based strategies to redesign their foundational history courses. The Gardner Institute has also been fortunate to work with the award-winning historian Edward Ayers and his colleague Annie Evans to scale the use of New American History. New American History provides history teachers with highly engaging digital scholarship tools, free of charge, to help students thrive in their history studies (New American History, 2020). As a recent article in *The Journal of American History* supports, these kinds of efforts help students see the purpose and relevance of American history to their daily lives, and this sense of purpose and relevance leads to much better outcomes (Ford et al., 2020). This is especially true for students who come from populations that have historically not done well in history courses.

In addition to discipline-based efforts, entire consortia of colleges and universities—two-year, four-year, public, and private/independent—are attempting to focus on efforts that lead to greater mastery of course content and deeper learning. Examples include the University System of Georgia's twenty-five-institution USG Gateways to Completion effort, the nine-institution Michigan Gateways to Completion effort conducted with help from the Michigan Center for Student Success and support from the Kresge Foundation, and the North Carolina Independent Colleges and Universities Gateways to Completion effort. As described in *Forbes*, Gateways to Completion is an effort undertaken by the Gardner Institute to help faculty work so that race/ethnic and family income are no longer the best predictors of who does or does not succeed in gateway courses (Nietzel, 2020).

Contrary to what deBoer claims, efforts such as these are not based on "cheery know-nothing optimism that insisted on seeing every student as an endlessly moldable lump of clay." Rather, they are evidence-based and equity-minded. They employ the kinds of active learning strategies that prompted Scott Freeman and his colleagues to write, in a June 2014 entry in *The Proceedings of the National Academies of Science,* that if experiments involving evidence-based strategies like those included in this essay "been conducted as randomized controlled trials of medical interventions, they may have been stopped for benefit—meaning that enrolling patients in the control condition might be discontinued because the treatment being tested was clearly more beneficial" (Freeman et al., 2014). Of greatest importance is that these kinds of efforts challenge allegiance to the assumptions that intellectual capacity is fixed, some students will always fail, and that we should be comfortable with this.

Debunking the Myths of Grades Curved and Inflated

One of the greatest limitations to thwarting the inequitable weed-out culture is a lack of imagination—an inability to ever see a possibility other than what exists right now. There are many who defend the weed-out status quo by asserting that they are maintaining cherished standards and defending their courses and disciplines from the ills of grade inflation. As the argument goes, grade inflation is the by-product of an emphasis on retention and completion. I have heard many academics assert in disgusted response to administrators talking about improving retention, "If you want to have higher retention rates, then just give everyone an A."

Let me be clear. Giving an A or a B or any grade to anyone who does not earn that grade is not just grade inflation, it is unethical. But let me also be clear, no course should have a predetermined and limited number of students who can earn an A or a guarantee that a certain percentage of students will always earn an F. Nowhere does this dynamic exist more than in courses that use curve grading.

Also referred to as *norm-referenced grading*—as grades are distributed along a normal distribution (curve)—curve grading compares a student's performance to other students in the same course. In other words, curve grading does not measure a mastery of content compared to a standard determined in advance by the instructor—such as a score of a 93 being the base threshold for an A, a score between 89 and 92 being an A–, and so on. That approach is called norm-referenced grading. Rather, instructors who use curve grading determine scores *after* students take the test by using a statistical technique to shape the distribution of grades into a bell curve. "An instructor then assigns a grade (e.g., C+) to the middle (median) score and determines grade thresholds based on the distance of scores from this reference point" (Reese, 2013).

Curve grading "widely practiced in foundational STEM (and many later) courses, tends to reify grades and detach them from their pedagogical purpose." Curve grading often leads to "misalignments between grades and the level of comprehension students thought they attained" (Seymour, Hunter, & Weston, 2019). It may be likely that the highest grade on an exam is a 72—an A in a curve grading schema compared to a much lower grade in a norm-referenced grading model.

Grading on a curve guarantees that there will be limitations of who can earn A grades. If, for example, all students earn at least or above a 90 on a 100-point exam, in a curve-grading schema students with a 90 would actually fail the test. That is the opposite of merit. It is grading by scare resource with the limited commodity being A grades. Curve grading also guarantees that there will absolutely be a fixed number of F grades—even if the F grade level in a current term could be equivalent to a passing grade in a previous semester. In other words, fixed and artificial standards limit possibilities—human possibilities. They also do not reflect content mastery very well.

What if courses were taught in such a way that A grades were possible for any and all students who earned them? No, not all courses use curve grading, but there are enough that do, and there are enough other high-stakes practices at work—feedback not coming until late in a term if at all, a few high-stakes assignments making up the bulk of the course grades, and so on—to show that weed-out culture is at the bedrock of the foundational experience in gateway courses in many, if not all, disciplines. Again, what if courses were structured and taught to eliminate these weed-out practices? In other words, what if we approached courses believing student ability can be improved and the faculty member was the prime guide for that process?

I've heard people tell me, in response to questions like the ones I just posed, that you cannot make an NFL-caliber starting quarterback out of someone who lacks any athletic ability. True enough—but that is an extreme argument and a false analogy. There are, at most, thirty-two athletes starting at quarterback on any given weekend during the NFL season. There are over ten million undergraduates in colleges and universities in the United States, and hundreds of millions of persons in the workforce.

We don't need faculty to create the equivalent of an NFL starting quarterback from all of their students. What we need are faculty who are appropriately prepared and supported so they can help more of the non-NFL-bound superstars master content in foundational courses so that those students, in turn, can help make up the predicted shortage of up to 139,000 physicians that the Association of American Medical Colleges projects the United States will face by 2033 (Boyle, 2020). We need faculty who can help more students master content in the STEM fields to help make up the projected shortfall of science, technology, and engineering professionals that the United States will face by 2030 if the country is to retain its historical preeminence in science and technology. This shortfall is projected to range between one million professionals, when considering a 2012 report released by the President's Council of Advisors on Science and Technology, and over 1.4 million, according to a 2023 summary shared by national defense industry experts (President's Council of Advisors on Science and Technology, 2012; Chase & Miles, 2023).

We don't need to winnow out learners unless they truly do not live up to growth- and mastery-oriented expectations we rightfully must set. Instead, we need to build them up. We are not trying to take below average athletes and turn them into Joe Montana or Patrick Mahomes. We are trying to help students who come from less resourced backgrounds—students who, against all odds, make it to college—master content in foundational courses so that they can succeed in fields that help address the aforementioned labor shortfalls. We are trying to help the same students break generation-spanning poverty cycles—for their well-being, the well-being of their families, and the health of the broader communities in which they will reside and to which they will contribute. Success in gateway courses is not the sole component needed to realize these lofty goals. But failure in gateway courses eliminates a great deal of the possibility thereof.

For those who think I am being hyperbolic, I refer you back to deBoer's essay. As part of his justification for maintaining the gateway course weed-out culture, deBoer writes:

> I've often said that our national conversation calls for colleges to chase two contradictory goals at once—higher standards, such as when people complain about grade inflation, and higher graduation rates. If we believe—and we should—that there are actual limits to how much students can learn and how effectively colleges can bring every student to the same proficiency level, then we also have to accept that we can have higher standards or higher graduation rates, but not both.

There is a big issue in deBoer's statement that must be addressed. That issue is the grade inflation narrative.

The grade inflation narrative assumes there are too many A grades or even too many passing grades. Thus, high achievement is a bad thing. This line of thinking advances the belief that the introductory course faculty member's primary role is not to educate students but to separate the wheat from the chaff. Otherwise, how would employers and graduate schools know who really deserved that coveted spot?

Yes, technically grades have gone up. But then there's the rest of the story . . .

According to research conducted by Rojstaczer and Healy since 2003, and currently including data collected from over 170 colleges and universities, grade point averages at four-year institutions have increased at a rate of 0.1 percentage points per decade. But grade point averages have remained flat at community colleges. While A grades have increased in four-year institutions, the rise is occurring while D and F grades remain stable. At community colleges, D and F grades have slightly increased, while A grades have dipped a bit. So, while there may be more A grades overall in the study sample, the frequency of the grade varies by sector, and the increases have not come as the result of fewer D and F grades (Rojstaczer & Healy, 2016; Jaschik, 2016).

Despite this evidence, we see countless headlines about grade inflation in the national media. For example, an article in *Forbes* argued that "Grade Inflation Is Not a Victimless Crime" (Hess, 2023), and an op-ed in *The Wall Street Journal* made the case that "Grade Inflation Makes the A the New C" (Wall Street Journal, 2023). With the use of phrases such as "participation trophies," "sheltered," and even "race to the bottom," the authors opine about how higher education has lost its way as a result of its increasing propensity to dole out As. Never mind the fact that even a brief examination of the data would not support the rampant hyperbole. And while the *New York Times* might print an article decrying the fact that nearly 80% of students at Yale get an A, that Harvard is not far behind, and that Princeton has done away with capping A grades (Nierenberg, 2023), calmer heads point out that what is going on at places like Yale "is simply compression: Yale is simply awarding more As because more Yale students are better prepared to genuinely earn As" (Hanlon, 2024).

In short, there is scant proof that grade inflation is actually happening at scale if at all. But this has not stopped some critics of grade inflation to place the blame for the trend and many other "problems we see plaguing our colleges" on "the passage of the Higher Ed Act of 1965," which came in the wake of the Civil Rights Act of 1964 (Wall Street Journal, 2023). This is a less-than-thinly veiled jab of Federal policy that expanded access to and the diversification of higher education in the United States over the past sixty years.

Much of the grade inflation criticism seems to rely on a similar foundational argument. If everyone gets an A, how will employers ever know who to hire and/or who to reject? I have news for you, they seem to be doing just fine. They are not having issues sorting through all those A students.

In an article published by the American Educational Research Association's journal, *Education Researcher*, Pattison, Grodsky, and Muller share the findings of their National Science Foundation–funded analysis of over twenty years of data on what they call "the signaling power of grades." Signaling power is defined as the ability of employers to use grades as a means for identifying talent. Noting at least a century-long narrative about "grades are not what they used to be," the authors share that while mean grades did rise over the period studied, "(c)ontrary to much of the existing literature, we find virtually no support for the existence of grade inflation in secondary or postsecondary education." The authors then add, "Furthermore, we do not observe any statistically significant attenuation in the signaling power of grades over this time period. In fact, we find some evidence of an *increase* in the signaling power of grades (Pattison, Grodsky, & Muller, 2013).

In other words, employers see a bit more value in the A grades now than they saw at the onset of the period studied. Employers are not confused by what to do with all those A students. We should not be confused either.

Final Thoughts—Weeding Out Our Weed-Out Predilections

About a week after my response to the deBoer essay was published in the *Chronicle Review*, I received a polite albeit disturbing message from an engineering professor who had read my essay. He wrote to let me know that he disagreed with my thinking, a good deal of which forms the basis for this chapter. Noting that he sympathized with my motives, he nevertheless felt compelled to disagree with my assertions. He felt compelled to let me know that his disagreement was based on a defense of his profession and the safety and well-being of people who drive across bridges.

His email was no incoherent rant. It was articulate. And firm. He let me know that he disagreed with my argument and motives, and implied that I lacked the wisdom that came with the responsibilities he shouldered in his role. He presented his case like a kinder and gentler version of Colonel Jessup—the antagonist of Aaron Sorkin's stage play *A Few Good Men*, who was portrayed by Jack Nicholson in the play's 1992 film adaptation.[1] When interrogated about the death of a Marine named Santiago by Lieutenant Daniel Kaffee, the Navy lawyer played by Tom Cruise, Jessup barked back that he had responsibilities to protect people that Kaffee could never fully comprehend. These responsibilities may require Jessup to behave in manners that Kaffee might deem grotesque but doing so saved lives. Thus, Kaffee should not just want Jessup to weed out weak Marines, he needed him to do so.

To be clear, I am not drawing a direct equivalence between the murder of a Marine ordered by his base commander and the intentional winnowing out of students by a professor. But I am pointing out the similarities in the arguments. Both the professor and the Colonel felt they had a duty to society that required them to make choices about who does or who does not get to remain in a group. Both conveyed that their decisions, while sometimes distasteful, were necessary because they guaranteed the safety of the greater whole—one with secure walls, the other with sturdy bridges.

It merits a mention that to become an engineer who designs bridges that don't fall down, a student must complete a four-year engineering degree. Then they must "work under a Professional Engineer for at least four years, pass two intensive competency exams and earn a license from their state's licensure board." There are added requirements from licensure boards for the bridge engineers to retain their licenses throughout their careers (National Society of Professional Engineers, 2024).

In other words, it is not an individual faculty member's responsibility to determine who does or does not get to build bridges. That responsibility belongs to state licensure boards following a rigorous preparation and examination process that spans years after college. However, it *is* an individual faculty member's responsibility to develop the talents of persons who could pass the licensure exam. Somehow this aspect of the argument was missed by the professor who emailed me.

I am not blaming that faculty member or any faculty members for the dynamics I am describing this this chapter. Rather, I am once again naming faculty as the best agents for the change for which I am advocating. We must support faculty to see what the system is actually doing, and then support them even more as they work to weed out the weed-out culture.

Undoubtedly, the challenges that confront higher education institutions and the educators who work in them are complex. The hard work of teaching and educational transformation has been made even harder due to inequitable conditions associated with the global pandemic and the learning loss that will plague students and educators for years to come. There are students, no matter what we do, that we will not be able to reach or teach in the moments we may have with them. But this does not mean we should view talent as fixed or see one of our primary roles as educators as "signaling value to employers" about the students our institutions have admitted. If we are resistant to the equity implications of the work we do and the untested assumptions surrounding that work, we will simply reproduce the inequitable structures that lie at the foundation of the institutions we serve.

Students are not seeds with some predetermined genetic size and yield. Evidence-based and equity-minded practices can be used in increasingly sophisticated ways—methods that consider multiple measures and that can, contrary to what Mr. deBoer asserted, lead to dramatic improvement.

If this chapter has done anything, I hope it has encouraged readers to check their own assumptions about fixed intellect, who does or does not belong in college, and why foundational courses need to perpetuate the weed-out culture. Doing so can result in not only improved outcomes for your students but also the broader democratic republic in which we all live and to which we all contribute.

Note

1 Reiner, R. (Director). (1992). *A Few Good Men*. Columbia Pictures.

References

Adelman, C. (1999). *Answers in the toolbox: Academic intensity, attendance patterns, and bachelor's degree attainment*. Washington, DC: US Department of Education, Office of Educational Research and Improvement.

Adelman, C. (2006). *The toolbox revisited: Paths to degree completion from high school through college*. Washington, DC: US Department of Education, Office of Educational Research and Improvement.

American Historical Association. (2019). *History gateways*. Washington, DC. Retrieved from https://www.historians.org/historygateways

Bagg, L. H. (1871). *Four years at Yale*. New Haven, CT: Charles C. Chattfield.

Boyle, P. (2020). *U.S. physician shortage growing*. Washington, DC: Association of American Medical Colleges. Retrieved from https://www.aamc.org/news/us-physician-shortage-growing

Chase, J., & Miles, W. (2023, October 27). Leveraging America's diverse STEM talent. *National Defense: NDIA's Business and Technology Magazine*. Retrieved from https://www.nationaldefensemagazine.org/articles/2023/10/27/emerging-technology-horizons-leveraging-americas-diverse-stem-talent

deBoer, F. (2020, August 27). Some students are smarter than others. (And that's ok): We should admit that not all students have the talent to succeed in college. *The Chronicle of Higher Education*

Review. Retrieved from https://www.chronicle.com/article/some-students-are-smarter-than-others-and-thats-ok

Ford, B., Chilton, K., Endy, C., Henderson, M., Jones, B. A., & Son, J. Y. (2020). Beyond big data: Teaching introductory US history in the age of student success. *Journal of American History, 106*(4), 989–1011.

Freeman, S., Eddy, S. L., McDonough, M., Smith, M. K., Okoroafor, N., Jordt, H., & Wenderoth, M. P. (2014). Active learning increases student performance in science, engineering, and mathematics. *Proceedings of the National Academy of Sciences, 111*(23), 8410–8415.

Grawe, N. D. (2018). *Demographics and the demand for higher education*. JHU Press.

Grawe, N. D. (2021). *The agile college: How institutions successfully navigate demographic changes*. JHU Press.

Hanlon, A. R. (2024, February). I know why college grades are going up. It's definitely not wokeism. *The New Republic*. Retrieved from https://newrepublic.com/article/178657/grade-inflation-college-not-wokeism

Hess, F. (2023, September 5). Grade inflation is not a victimless crime. *Forbes*. Retrieved from https://www.forbes.com/sites/frederickhess/2023/09/05/grade-inflation-is-not-a-victimless-crime

Jaschik, S. (2016, March 26). Grade inflation, higher and higher: The most common grade is A—At all kinds of colleges. But while grade point averages are increasing at four-year institutions, that's not the case at community colleges. *Inside Higher Ed*. Retrieved from https://www.insidehighered.com/news/2016/03/29/survey-finds-grade-inflation-continues-rise-four-year-colleges-not-community-college

King, M. L., Jr. (2010). *Where do we go from here: Chaos or community?* (Vol. 2). Boston, MA: Beacon Press.

Koch, A. K. (2017). Many thousands failed: A wakeup call to history educators. *Perspectives on History, 55*(5), 18–19.

Koch, A. K., & Drake, B. M. (2018). *Digging into the disciplines I: Accounting for failure—The impact of principles of accounting courses on student success and equitable outcomes*. Brevard, NC: John N. Gardner Institute for Excellence in Undergraduate Education.

Koch, A. K., & Drake, B. M. (2019). *Digging into the disciplines II: Failure in historical context—The impact of introductory U.S. history courses on student success and equitable outcomes*. Brevard, NC: John N. Gardner Institute for Excellence in Undergraduate Education.

National Society of Professional Engineers. (2024). *What is PE?* Retrieved from https://www.nspe.org/resources/licensure/what-pe

New American History. (2020). Retrieved from https://www.newamericanhistory.org/

Nierenberg, A. (2023, December 6). Excellence at Yale doubted as nearly everyone gets A's. *The New York Times*, Section A, p. 21.

Nietzel, M. T. (2020, February 6). College initiatives for 2020, part IV: Want to improve student success? Start by improving introductory courses. *Forbes*. Retrieved from https://www.forbes.com/sites/michaeltnietzel/2020/02/06/college-initiatives-for-2020-part-iv-transforming-the-large-introductory-course/

Pattison, E., Grodsky, E., & Muller, C. (2013). Is the sky falling? Grade inflation and the signaling power of grades. *Educational Researcher*, 42(5), 259–265.

President's Council of Advisors on Science and Technology. (2012). *Engage to excel: Producing 1 million additional college graduates with degrees in science, technology, engineering, and mathematics*. Retrieved from https://obamawhitehouse.archives.gov/sites/default/files/microsites/ostp/pcast-engage-to-excel-final_2-25-12.pdf

Purdue University Data Digest. (2020). Retrieved from https://www.purdue.edu/datadigest/

Quay, L., & Romero, C. (2020). What we know about learning mindsets from scientific research. *Mindset Scholars Network*. Retrieved from https://studentexperiencenetwork.org/wp-content/uploads/2015/09/What-We-Know-About-Learning-Mindsets.pdf

Reese, M. J. (2013). *To curve of not to curve (The innovative instructor)*. Johns Hopkins University Center for Teaching Excellence and Innovation. Retrieved from https://ctei.jhu.edu/files/ii-bp-08_to-curve-or-not-to-curve.pdf

Rojstaczer, S., & Healy, C. (2016, March 29). *Grade inflation at American colleges and universities*. Retrieved from https://www.gradeinflation.com/

Schinske, J., & Tanner, K. (2014). Teaching more by grading less (or differently). *CBE—Life Sciences Education*, 13(2), 159–166.

Schneider, J., & Hutt, E. (2014). Making the grade: A history of the A–F marking scheme. *Journal of Curriculum Studies*, 46(2), 201–224.

Seale, A. (2019, September 19). No left side of the curve: David Laude battles deeply ingrained notions at the intersection of education and social justice. *UT News*. Retrieved from https://news.utexas.edu/2019/09/19/no-left-side-of-the-curve/

Seymour, E., Hunter, A.-B., & Weston, T. J. (2019). Why are we still talking about leaving? In E. Seymour & A.-B. Hunter (Eds.), *Talking about leaving revisited: Persistence, relocation, and loss in undergraduate STEM education* (pp. 1–53). New York: Springer Publishing Company.

Shrider, E. (2023). *Black individuals had record low official poverty rate in 2022*. Washington, DC: Unite States Census Bureau. Retrieved from https://www.census.gov/library/stories/2023/09/black-poverty-rate.html

Smallwood, M. L. (1935). *An historical study of examinations and grading systems in early American universities: A critical study of the original records of Harvard, William and Mary, Yale, Mount Holyoke, and Michigan from their founding to 1900*. Cambridge, MA: Harvard University Press.

Stewart, D. L. (2020). Twisted at the roots: The intransigence of inequality in US higher education. *Change: The Magazine of Higher Learning, 52*(2), 13–16.

Student Experience Research Network. (2023). Retrieved from https://studentexperiencenetwork.org/

Wall Street Journal. (2023). Grade inflation makes A the New C. (2023, December 19). Retrieved from https://www.wsj.com/articles/grade-inflation-makes-a-the-new-c-participation-trophy-quiet-quitting-hiring-2c480b80

Westin, T. J., Seymour, E., Koch, A. K., & Drake, B. M. (2020). Weed-out classes and their consequences. In E. Seymour & A.-B. Hunter (Eds.), *Talking about leaving revisited: Persistence, relocation, and loss in undergraduate STEM education* (pp. 207–259). New York: Springer Publishing Company.

5

Taking Action—A Three-Phase Model for Gateway Course Redesign

This last chapter presents a three-phase model for gateway course redesign that the Gardner Institute, the organization I am privileged to serve, has used with nearly 100 colleges and universities to date. Educators across all types of postsecondary institutions can apply this model, with or without the help of the Gardner Institute, to make sure that demographics are not destiny in gateway courses and postsecondary educational experiences of which those courses are a part. Admittedly, this is a long chapter—the longest of the book. But it is necessarily long—as gateway course redesign is no small task, and thus approaches to addressing the issues should not suffer from short shrift.

A Brief Overview of the Model

In 2013, the Gardner Institute launched an initiative called Gateways to Completion (G2C). The work evolved organically from other Gardner Institute efforts up to that time—work that helped institutions redesign the first year and/or the transfer experiences. Between 1999 and 2012, the findings from that work clearly suggested that colleges and universities would only be successful in improving student learning and completion outcomes if, in addition to their work on the first college year and transfer, they intentionally focused on how students were performing in gateway courses. Thus, G2C was born as an evidence-based process for creating and implementing plans for improving student learning and success in courses that have historically resulted in high rates of failure for students.

High failure rate courses are identified by their rates of D, F, W for withdrawal, and I for incomplete grades. Generally, institutions choose to focus on redesign of courses that have high "DFWI rates" and enroll a large number of students either within or across course sections. These courses are a challenge for all students, but especially take their toll on students of color, students from low-income families, and students who are the first in their families to go to college (Koch, 2017; Koch & Drake, 2018, 2019).

The G2C process must be understood as an effort that helps educators focus on and improve what happens at the nexus of the student success and equity imperatives. Since its launch in 2013, nearly 100 colleges and universities have been involved in the G2C effort. This includes two- and four-year, public and private, not-for-profit, and proprietary institutions enrolling over one million undergraduates.

Three distinct phases make up the G2C course redesign process. The first—the "Analyze and Plan" phase—is essentially a self-study process that helps educators gather evidence, analyze that evidence, and, as a result, create a set of recommendations—a plan—for improving student learning and success in one or more gateway courses that are the focus of the effort. The second phase of the work—the "Act and Monitor" phase—is the stage in which educators first implement the plan. The third phase of the effort—"Continued Action and Refinement"—is the period where, based on what was learned through experience in the "Act and Monitor" stage, educators further refine their course redesign.

Phase I: Analyze and Plan

In case the name did not give it away, the Analyze and Plan phase—Phase I—is all about analyzing evidence and using the results of that analysis to create a set of recommendations that instructors implement. Phase I can be broken down into four main components. These include (A) organizing people for the work; (B) collecting evidence; (C) analyzing evidence; and (D) generating an initial plan. Details associated with each of the four components, as well as some general overarching thoughts about supporting the work in this phase, follow.

A. Organizing People for the Work

Course redesign should not be an isolated effort left to one person. If the work is attempted this way, the effort is destined to fail. That is not a criticism of stalwart individuals. Rather, it is an acknowledgment that courses, by their very nature, exist in broader institutional ecosystems. There are many policies, practices, and dynamics that influence outcomes in courses that are well beyond the control of an individual instructor. In short, it takes a village to redesign a course; and that village needs to be thoughtfully organized to launch, operate, and sustain the challenging work.

The Gardner Institute advises institutions to create a task force for course redesign. While approaches will vary, the task force generally consists of project leaders, a steering committee, and course-specific committees. Course-specific committees carry out significant portions of the work. My Gardner Institute colleagues and I advise institutions, in general, to create a course-specific committee for each course the institution is redesigning.

Each committee should be led by a chair and comprised of educators responsible for student learning and success in the course that is being transformed. Note I used the term "educators." While course committees should absolutely include the course instructors, there are other educators—academic advisors, department heads, institutional research staff, faculty developers, student success program staff, and so on—who also contribute to and inform teaching, learning, and success in the classroom. These kinds of educators have insight that is vital to course redesign efforts.

In addition, in many cases, non-tenure-track instructors teach sections—often most of the sections—of a given course. Their experiences are too important to leave out of the course committee work. Some academic administrators have told me that part-time, non-tenure-track instructors are routinely involved in course redesign efforts and are paid for their efforts.

In the case of smaller institutions—where one person or two people teach all the sections of a specific course—it may make sense to have one large committee that spans multiple courses. This keeps the work manageable and makes course redesign the responsibility of a broader set of educators, not just the one or two faculty who would otherwise do the course redesign work.

At medium-to-larger institutions, in addition to having course committee chairs, the Gardner Institute recommends that at least two persons be tabbed as the overall project leaders. These leaders are responsible for oversight of the committee chairs, the compilation of a broader report that seeks to harmonize findings and recommendations across courses when and where feasible, and coordination with institutional research and other entities. The project leaders also chair a cross-course steering committee that is populated by the various committee chairs. This project steering committee provides a structure for the synthesis of findings and recommendations.

Even the largest of institutions will have staff limitations. For example, an institution may have many instructors teaching sections of a specific course and many full-time advisors. But in all likelihood that institution will have one institutional research office with a few staff as well as one tutoring program also with a few professional staff members. Rather than attending multiple course committee meetings, those smaller units can work through the cross-course steering committee to provide essential information to each particular committee.

B. Collecting Evidence

With the task force populated—and perhaps even before it is fully constructed—institutions should set out to gather the evidence that is needed to do this work. Otherwise, the "evidence-based" process will be "evidence-free" and continue the perpetuation of myths and misunderstandings that harm students—especially students of color, low-income, and first-generation college students. The evidence takes four basic forms. These include:

1. Historic Gateway Course Data/Analytics

I am not boasting when I write that my colleagues and I could write a whole chapter—perhaps even a book—on just the kinds of data that are necessary for the equitable redesign of gateway courses at postsecondary institutions. This is not that book. However, it merits mentioning now that no course redesign effort can be successful if it does not include actual historic student performance data in the course.

We recommend that DFWI rates be shared both in aggregate for each course and disaggregated by specific populations and characteristics. Common disaggregated outputs for DFWI rates include race/ethnicity, gender, family income (we use Pell grant status as a proxy for family income), first-generation standing, and academic standing (first-year student, transfer, second-year student, etc.). In addition, it is often quite useful to disaggregate DFWI rates by classification of the instructor—tenured/tenure track, adjunct, and so on.

Aggregate and disaggregated data on DFWI rates should also be linked to retention and graduation rate data. Doing so shows the correlation between earning an unsatisfactory grade in the course and retention to the next year and/or graduation over time. Educators are frequently shocked to see just how predictive even one low grade in a gateway course is for future retention and graduation outcomes. These kinds of responses and insights are missed if the data on grades are not connected to data on persistence and completion.

At two-year colleges, where associate degrees are the primary degree granted, data that connect DFWI rates with two- and three-year graduation rates is important. But it makes sense for two-year institutions to provide even more years of gateway course, retention, and graduation data. At four-year institutions, where four-, five-, and six-year graduation rates are the norm, we advise institutions to work with nine to ten years of data. While course committees can use the data from the most recent two to three years for the bulk of their work, they will need the long-term data to see the connection between course outcomes and persistence and completion over time.

Institutions should be mindful when they are sharing disaggregated data that include small population numbers— such as DFWI rates from a particularly small number of students or by instructor type when only a few people hold that instructor classification. This does not mean you should not share data for smaller populations—since even the smallest of numbers can be meaningful. But there are confidentiality issues with smaller numbers that must be handled thoughtfully so as not to violate educational privacy laws.

If possible, it is best to collect and share the data on all your courses. This allows the course committees to see evidence not just for their own course but contextualize their course's data with that from other courses. In addition, the act of collecting data on all courses may point out other opportunities for course redesign. This is particularly true when course outcomes are disaggregated as suggested before.

2. Surveys/Focus Groups of Current Students and Educators

The historic data mentioned in the previous section will show course committee members how well students in the past years did in specific courses. But that data won't share the perspectives of the current students enrolled in or the educators teaching the course. That perspective can be gleaned via surveys and/or focus groups.

Institutions may want to use a common set of questions when surveying and/or conducting focus groups with faculty, staff, and students. This will allow course committees to see if everyone is perceiving what is going on in the course in the same ways. This approach does not mean that all the questions need to be the same. But having some consistency does allow for the analysis of congruence and/or incongruence—which provide value when creating plans for continuous improvement.

In its work surveying students, the Gardner Institute makes use of questions derived from the Student Assessment of Learning Gains (SALG) survey (Seymour, Wiese, Hunter, & Daffinrud, 2000). We do so with the approval of the SALG team, and with deep gratitude to Dr. Elaine Seymour who first developed the instrument in 1997. Dr. Seymour did so while serving as co-evaluator for two National Science Foundation–funded chemistry consortia (ChemLinks and ModularCHEM). In 2007, Dr. Seymour worked with colleagues Dr. Stephen Carroll (an English professor) and Tim Weston (a research scientist at the University of Colorado Boulder) to revise the SALG so that it better reflected the goals and methods of a broader array of STEM and other courses—not just chemistry.

One of the many things my Gardner Institute colleagues and I like about the SALG is that the instrument focuses exclusively on the degree to which students perceive that a course has enabled their learning. Specifically, the SALG asks students to report on their own learning, and on the ways in which specific features of a course—particularly pedagogical approaches used by faculty—have contributed to that learning. The current instrument focuses on five overarching questions. These questions can be customized by individual instructors to reflect how they are teaching the course. These five questions essentially explore:

(1) The degree to which the aspects of a course help students learn. (Some examples of aspects include quizzes, resources, lab activities, etc.)
(2) The perceived gains in learning that students made as a result of what they did in the course. (Instructors identify and insert the concepts they deem most important.)
(3) The perceived gains in skills that students made as a result of what they did in the course. (An instructor can include skills like writing, quantitative analysis, speaking, etc.)
(4) The perceived gains in attitudes and beliefs as a result of what students did in the course. (An example of this is increased interest in the course or field.)
(5) The degree to which the course helped students integrate various forms of learning they encountered in other parts of their educational experience.

The fact that the SALG is focused on perceived gains in learning that are related to teaching strategies is particularly helpful in a course redesign effort. This is because analyzing evidence such as DFWI rates alone may make some people think that the effort is all about giving more passing grades without verifying that learning is occurring. That is the antithesis of why this work is being done. Grades should reflect content mastery and learning in the course—even if they are a proxy for those outcomes. Analysis of SALG outcomes is one way to make sure that the course redesign effort is linked with teaching and learning.

Use of the SALG isn't essential. But you should use a form of evidence—a survey tool or focus group structure or even both—that garners current perspectives from the students who are taking, and faculty and staff engaged in the delivery of, the course. And that evidence should be squarely focused on teaching and learning.

3. Inventories of Current Practices, Policies, and Committees

Inventories of current course-related structures are another important source of evidence for course redesign efforts. We recommend that an institution undergoing a course redesign effort inventory at least three forms of information. These include (1) current practices; (2) policies; and (3) committees.

An inventory of current practices should include academic support programs of all types. It is important when inventorying current practices to share whether participation is voluntary or universal/mandatory—and, if mandatory, for whom the engagement is required.

Inventories of policies should include general policies that impact teaching, learning, and success in gateway courses such as those associated with academic advising, late registration, add/drop, satisfactory academic progress, academic honors, academic probation, and financial aid. Other course-specific policies include prerequisites, attendance, grading, and requirements of persons who are employed to instruct the course. An institution may also want to share how faculty work on improving teaching and learning in gateway courses gets factored into tenure and promotion.

An inventory of committees should include any committee that has direct or indirect implications for successful teaching and learning in courses and the related programs of study. Examples include curricular committees, education policy committees, and committees that recognize and reward instructors for exemplary teaching and scholarship on teaching and learning.

The importance of the committee inventory cannot be underestimated—as these committees may "make or break" course redesign efforts. Consideration should be given to how committees that appear on the inventory are involved in and informed about course redesign efforts. In addition, given that time and effort are precious resources, serious consideration—with appropriate follow-up actions—should be given by institutional leaders to the way course redesign efforts can "count" as committee or service contributions by the faculty who are involved.

The examples shared here are not the only kinds of structures that you can include in your inventory. But they should give you a good start on the types of practices, policies, and committee structures you will want to factor into your gateway course redesign evidence collection efforts.

4. Other Forms of Evidence

Other forms of evidence include any kinds of research or scholarship that your faculty and staff have produced on teaching, learning, and success in gateway courses. Examples include work done on gateway course redesign in national projects such as those facilitated by the Howard Hughes Medical Institute, scholarship on teaching and learning that your faculty and/or staff may have published or presented, and reports about or dashboards associated with gateway course success generated by your institutional research staff.

These other forms of evidence should be included because they allow your "local experts" to meaningfully contribute to and engage in the course redesign work. In short, applying the scholarship and research of your local experts allows you to build "a bigger tent."

An Additional Thought on Evidence

I would be remiss if I failed to note that none of the forms of evidence is "better" than the others. In addition, I also must point out that it may not be possible for institutions to gather all the forms of evidence I suggest. What is important is that institutions use the evidence they have to redesign their courses as best as they can, and that the evidence that is being used is considered collectively. In other words, it is the weight of the evidence that matters, not the supremacy of one form of evidence compared to another.

C. Analyzing the Evidence

With evidence collected, institutions are ready to move on to evidence analysis. We have learned in our gateway course redesign work at the Gardner Institute that this phase of the work is most productive if course committees use a common framework to consider and apply the evidence. The Gardner Institute created and refined a set of six overarching principles that provide this framework:

(1) Learning
(2) Academic Policy and Practice
(3) Faculty/Instructors
(4) Improvement
(5) Students
(6) Support

We placed the Learning principle first—to make it abundantly clear that course redesign efforts should be about improved learning, and not about "giving everyone an A." For the same reasons we put Learning first, we placed Academic Policy and Practice and Faculty/Instructors next—to place the focus on how teaching, and those who teach, are supported. The Improvement principle should be understood as the way institutions support the collection, dissemination, and application of evidence to improve teaching, learning, and success in gateway courses. We placed the Student and Support principles last because while we believe that it is vital for faculty and staff to know about the students who take their courses, we do not want to start with a close examination of students as the first lens for analysis. This helps educators avoid the temptation of blaming students for design issues, or simply adding more "out-of-class" supports without prior insight and reflection.

A framework like the six principles is necessary but insufficient. Any framework can yield the desired outcomes only if it is supported with key performance indicators (KPIs) that expose issues and suggest possibilities. Because of this, the Gardner Institute has created approximately fifty KPIs that it uses across the six principles—with each principle having somewhere between six and ten related KPIs. The key performance indicators are presented as an opportunity for course committees to rate—not rank—course-level performance. Here I must note the difference between a rating and a ranking. In my experience, rankings are a zero-sum game that leads to a few winners—perhaps only one—and many losers. Ratings are about both current and future states of excellence and they allow room for all. In other words, ratings allow all educators to reflect on the current performance in a specific area and discuss possibilities for better states of performance.

The promise of ratings is amplified when the rating exercise is informed by evidence. To make the evidence-based rating process possible, the Gardner Institute has linked the evidence collected in the historic data analysis, the inventories, and surveys to specific principles and KPIs associated therewith. This helps busy educators quickly sort through what can otherwise be a voluminous set of evidence.

D. Creating an Initial Plan

In the process of reviewing evidence and rating institutional performance with the KPIs, the course committees will invariably identify actions that they will undertake to improve performance in the course. These recommendations should be captured, in writing, and then reviewed by the course-specific committee once all ratings are completed. This review is done so that the course-specific committee can create a prioritized plan of action—a course redesign plan that is based on and supported by review of evidence. In many cases, this course-specific redesign plan is formally developed into a polished plan of action.

When institutions undertake course redesign across multiple courses at the same time, efforts should be made by course committee chairs and project leaders to synthesize the recommendations. Doing so allows the institution—particularly the steering committee—to identify cross-course recommendations.

I have seen institutions that undertake this work produce and disseminate very polished reports that show both what was learned by the educators involved in the work and what they will now do based on what they learned. But regardless of the approach to dissemination, the plans should be implemented. Failure to do so not only hurts future efforts of this nature but also allows unjust outcomes to perpetuate and perhaps even grow. In short, for institutional effectiveness and moral reasons, you must implement the plans you generate.

Phase II—Implementing the Plan

Why Focus on Implementation?

The first phase of the three-phase course redesign process described previously is all about gathering and analyzing evidence to "face as much of the truth" as educators can bear about gateway courses and outcomes at their own institutions. The goal of the first phase is to help educators create evidence-based plans to achieve more equitable student learning and success in their gateway courses. Now we must move to implementing (Phase 2) and refining (Phase 3) that plan. I also want to provide some examples of what educators did as a result of generating and refining their plans, and the outcomes of those actions.

In our work at the Gardner Institute, I and my colleagues have found that postsecondary educators are very good at conducting self-studies and generating plans from that process. Sadly, we have also found that many of those educators fall short of being excellent when it comes to implementing the plans they generate.

For example, let's consider the results of the external analysis that examined the work of over 130 institutions that participated in Gardner Institute initiatives to redesign the totality of the first college year. The cohort included institutions of all types—two-year, four-year, public, and private. Broadly these colleges and universities were open access or moderately selective institutions. On average, the institutions (both two- and four-year) recorded a 3-percentage point increase in IPEDS (Integrated Postsecondary Education Data System) first- to second-year retention rates over a four-year period spanning the end of the planning and start of the implementation effort (Drake, 2010). Similar results were found when examining community colleges as a subset of the overall cohort (Drake, 2011).

As part of the analysis, the external evaluator asked institutions to report the degree to which they implemented their plans according to these four categories: (1) no implementation, (2) low implementation, (3) medium implementation, and (4) high implementation. Institutions that self-reported that they implemented their plans to a high degree saw the greatest gains in IPEDS retention rates—a 5.62 percentage point (8.2%) increase (Drake, 2010). The retention rate increases translated into significant gains in retention-related revenue and over a $26 return on their investment in the particular initiative (Drake, 2011).

The evaluation also revealed that institutions reporting any other degree of implementation—no degree, low degree, and even medium degree—experienced attrition over the period of the study. In other words, generating a plan but failing to implement it to anything but a high degree resulted in decreases in institutional retention rates.

In summary:

- You have to create a plan.
- Then you have to implement the plan.
- And you have to implement that plan to a high degree.

Moving from Planning to Implementing

Implementation takes time. Dr. Leo Lambert, President Emeritus of Elon University and a member of the Gardner Institute's board of directors, once told me that it takes ten years to get hard things done. Creating, successfully implementing, and then sustaining gateway course redesigns is hard. Institutions must commit to hard work ahead. Based on our research, the missing pieces associated with implementation had very little to do with money. In fact, only one institution reported not being able to implement due to lack of resources for their plan. Leadership—specifically leadership changes—was the issue. Not just an issue. *The* issue.

But providing structure, assuring commitment, and creating broad leadership for change are all things that institutions can control. Not only can they control for these factors, but they must also control for them if they are going to be successful in implementing plans of any kind including plans for gateway course redesign. What follows are some recommendations for you to consider as you move from planning to implementation—so that your institution can be a "high implementer" and derive the associated benefits.

Building and Sustaining Structure to Successfully Implement Gateway Course Redesign Plans

Growing a successful course redesign effort is like growing cucumbers—you need to provide good structure (a trellis) to support the effort, and even when you have that structure and the work is firmly rooted, you must continue to feed and water the endeavor for it to yield fruit. Leadership is one of the most important nutrients in starting, growing, and sustaining a course redesign process.

Colleges and universities will often convert the members of their self-study task force into their plan implementation team for the resulting plans. This makes sense, as the persons who helped generate the plans are well informed about the "hows and whys" that led to the recommended actions. If new people are brought into the implementation team, careful support should be given so that they don't spend most of their early time trying to "re-do" the self-study.

The term leadership should be understood broadly. Mirroring what was done with the self-study task force, there are opportunities for implementation leadership at the course and cross-course levels as well as on the steering committee. The cross-course task force leadership roles should be given to at least two or more persons. Academic affairs, faculty, and student success leaders—and/or the people who immediately report to them—often serve in these roles. In course-level leadership there will be at least two, if not more, faculty who are responsible for overseeing the implementation of the plans generated by each of the course-specific committees. Institutional research, student support, and academic advising staff often provide additional leadership for implementation at the steering committee level.

I am emphasizing leadership—especially distributed leadership—to counteract what happens when one or a few persons are leading a course redesign effort. Remember the findings from the implementation research shared previously—low implementation and low performance are directly correlated with leadership transition. Thus, it is wise not to make this "the Provost's" or "the Dean's" course redesign effort—at least not in a way that solely identifies the effort with one person or leader. Rather, it is wise to go into the implementation work understanding that there will be some transition—it is inevitable. People's lives change. They may receive an offer they cannot refuse, opt to retire, or take a well-deserved sabbatical. They might even win Powerball—even if the odds are ridiculously low, someone eventually does win. Those changes do not have to derail your course redesign efforts if you distribute the leadership broadly to develop both current and future leaders at the institution.

The significance of leadership development cannot be overstated. My Gardner Institute colleagues and I know of several persons who headed self-study teams, moved into leadership for the implementation of the plans that were generated, and over time became senior leaders at the institutions where they did the redesign work. Will you be your college or university's future president or chief academic officer by taking on self-study and implementation leadership now? While there are no guarantees, doing so does not seem to hurt the odds. And those odds are better than winning the Powerball jackpot.

In addition to leadership, there are at least four other forms of support that institutions need to address to successfully launch their plan implementation. These include: (1) overall project management structures, (2) plan implementation monitoring and reporting tools, (3) communication and celebration strategies, and (4) faculty development. A few thoughts on each of these four elements follow:

- ♦ Use a project management structure/approach

    Not knowing where or how to move from generating recommendations to actually implementing them has surfaced as a reason for not being able to implement to a high degree. In other words, sometimes people just don't know how to start in moving from planning to doing. Because this is not uncommon, structures exist to help launch and then continuously advance the implementation process.

    Specifically, there is a growing body of scholarship on, and tools that support, project management. Whether drawing on improvement science, implementation science, or any other form of change management theory, the basic premise is essentially the same—good management structures and techniques tend to help organizations advance even the hardest of changes. In other words, project management provides the structure and means for keeping a change process in motion.

    My Gardner Institute colleagues and I have generated templates for task forces to use to help them move from the planning to the initial implementation phase of the work. The templates break down larger recommendations into actionable tasks, with considerations such as timelines, personnel, evaluation, and funding factored in. While the templates are helpful, the end users look at what we provide and then adapt it to their own context.

    One common way for advancing implementation is through the use of project management software. The Gardner Institute is project management software agnostic. In other words, we are not biased toward the use of any specific software to solve institutional plan implementation challenges. If you like Asana, use it. If you like Microsoft Project, use it. If you like Monday, use it. And if you prefer carrier pigeons and semaphores, use them. In short, you don't only need to have a plan. You need to have an approach for implementing that plan—and that approach should factor in sound project management strategies and tools.

- Create, monitor, and report project-related metrics

Part of the project management plan must include the means for monitoring and sharing project results for purposes of ongoing learning and improvement. The creation and ongoing monitoring of project metrics must consider the same dynamics discussed earlier in this chapter about gateway course evidence—namely that it can get really personal really fast. Thus, there may be the need for various levels of metrics and reporting with some reporting being limited to an individual while other forms being shared more broadly. All of it should be firmly rooted in and promoted as a culture of continuous improvement—with improvement being expressed (often) as eliminating race/ethnicity and family income as the best predictors of who succeeds in a gateway course.

Like the initial self-study process that yielded the plan, implementation metrics will need to draw from both qualitative and quantitative sources. For example, making use of and comparing SALG results along with course outcomes themselves on a longitudinal basis will give consistent measures over a multi-year implementation process. However, course outcomes such as aggregate and disaggregated grades will only go so far as they are summative in nature. For this reason, be sure to factor in a combination of short-term/leading indicators (such as results from early feedback, early assignment grades, etc.) with intermediate measures (such as the course grades and SALG outcomes) and lagging indicators (such as retention and graduation rates) into the monitoring and reporting plan.

Dashboards always seem to come up when the topic of metrics and reporting comes up. As with project management software, my Gardner Institute colleagues and

I are dashboard brand agnostic. Do you need them? Yes. And there are a variety of tools available—and some low-cost and even free ones have as much virtue as some of the high-cost options in the market depending on how you plan to use them. So, pick one and use it for your efforts. You can always change it as your needs evolve and circumstances indicate. That shared, once you have a dashboard tool, you must be prepared to answer the question, "We have dashboards, now what?" The answer to that question is found in how you help your community decide what is reported in the dashboard and use that output as part of a broader course redesign implementation effort.

- Create and implement a communication and recognition strategy

Building and scaling momentum for a course redesign effort is related to the degree to which people are even aware the work is going on. I have seen well-intended and highly motivated faculty give up on course redesign efforts when they feel as if they are doing the work in isolation and that no one notices or, worse yet, even cares. I encourage you to be very intentional about how you share news about the ongoing work—especially with the broader institutional community in which the courses are situated.

Convocations at the start of year and/or term are an excellent place to report on progress of the work and showcase exemplars. If you showcase the effort, everyone at the institution will get that this work really matters—especially the faculty and staff who are doing the "heavy lifting" associated with the effort.

In addition to public meetings, thoughtful inclusion about the effort on the institution's website, or in printed and social media also matters. For example, I was pleased to see that the University of Richmond highlighted the work of Elisabeth Gruner, professor of English—specifically her essay on her efforts with "ungrading" in undergraduate writing courses (Brown, 2022). Ungrading, a practice that has gained momentum since the onset of the pandemic, emphasizes learning over grades, especially on individual assignments within a course. To be clear, the University of Richmond has not worked with the Gardner Institute on its teaching and learning efforts, and the story it shared was reprinted from an essay originally published in both *The Conversation* (Gruner, 2022) and on the PBS NewsHour website (Gruner, 2022). But the University is clearly thinking about ways in which it can use its own communications—in this case, its monthly alumni magazine—to highlight and support faculty working to improve what goes on in the classroom.

The Gruner essay is just one example of how an institution can promote the work of educators working to improve equitable teaching and learning in undergraduate courses. These approaches can and should go beyond publicity—even if publicity is important. Project leaders should find ways to support the contributions that their faculty and staff make to the scholarship of teaching and learning—in scholarly journals or, like Gruner's example, in publications shared with a broader public. In addition, institutions should find the means to support their course redesign participants to present their work at regional, national, and even international convenings focused on teaching and learning.

Finally, project leaders should seek out opportunities to nominate their course redesign participants, either individually or collectively, for both internal and/or external awards. An example of this was the effort made by leadership at Eastern Michigan University (EMU) to recognize the institution's whole course redesign task force for its efforts in closing inequitable performance gaps in five different gateway courses. The EMU leadership submitted their project description and results for consideration for a statewide recognition for "Equity in Education" given by the Michigan Association of Collegiate Registrars and Admission Officers (MACRAO). The convincing, evidence-supported submission compelled the

MACRAO reviewers to award the Eastern Michigan task force the 2019 prize (MACRAO, 2019). Recognitions like these go a long way toward letting educators know that their efforts truly matter.

- Focus on faculty development

When we started our course redesign work in 2012, we focused on developing the best evidence-based self-study process we could build. What we avoided—based on our own insight but also based on the guidance we received from a national advisory committee was doing anything that hinted at or looked like we were telling the faculty what they had to do in their courses. All we wanted to do is provide a structure for the self-study process itself. We especially avoided anything that came across as pedagogical guidance—for fear that doing so would come across as a mandate to people who did not take mandates very well at all. In hindsight, this was a mistake.

We quickly learned from the faculty involved in the self-study work that, once presented with the evidence—particularly evidence about inequitable outcomes in the courses they taught—they wanted to learn about what they could do. Frequently we heard distressed responses like, "I never knew this. What can I do about it?!?" We realized we could no longer not provide an answer to that question. We had to provide support for learning about equity-minded, evidence-based pedagogies and applying them to course redesign efforts. But we needed to make sure that they were understood as part of the formula for course redesign—not the sole response to the question, "What can I do?" Thus, in 2014, we launched the first Teaching and Learning Academy (TLA). In early 2023, when I was writing this chapter, the TLA is on at least its fifth version—shifting to a hybrid model that allows broader access to contingent and part-time faculty, which our initial in-person workshops did not.

The important takeaway from our work on supporting faculty development is not how we are doing it. The key lesson is that we *are* doing it, and that it needs to be an intentional part of any credible course redesign effort. As mentioned in the previous paragraph, leading with faculty development—no matter how good the experience is—can lead instructors to jump to a priori decisions about what they should or should not do in their courses. Yet not providing support for faculty to learn about evidence-based pedagogies—the kind of support that many faculty never received in graduate school—can lead to all aspects of the course redesign being about what happens outside of and/or around the course.

There are many institutions that have robust or at least growing faculty development units. If yours is among them, these staff must be intentionally incorporated into the course redesign planning and implementation process. Yet, there are still many institutions that do not have these kinds of resources or have them on a limited basis—where faculty development is a brown bag series offered a few times a year. This is where external support from non-profit entities like the Gardner Institute or the Professional and Organizational Development Network in Higher Education (POD) or even from investor-backed ventures like the Association of College and University Educators may be of help.

Regardless of how you do it, you must factor in faculty development into your course redesign effort. Like the redesign itself, that development should be understood as a continuous enterprise—where evidence and experience with pedagogy always shape the ongoing refinement of teaching and learning in a course. Don't make our mistake. Be intentional with faculty development from the onset, especially as you move from planning into initial implementation of your course redesign plans.

Phase III: Continued Action and Refinement

This third phase of the course redesign process may be the least heralded. It may also be the most important—or at least the first among equals. This is the place where course redesign plans flourish or die.

In my work with course redesign since 2012, I've never known an initial plan that got things 100% correct before it was implemented. There are always miscalculations—theoretically sound thinking that does not stand the test of experience. Once the plans get implemented, educators must adapt to and overcome the challenges that inevitably arise when the plans make contact with classrooms. The challenges associated with doing so must not be underestimated.

In their first edition of *Talking About Leaving Revisited* (1997), Elaine Seymour and Nancy Hewitt pointed out that the STEM faculty do not fail to make use of evidence-based pedagogies because they do not know about them. Rather, they do not use those pedagogies because the faculty tried them once and experienced challenges when doing so. Rather than stick with the evidence-based strategies and refine their approaches, the STEM faculty went back to using traditionally didactic methods—methods associated with the disproportionate "weeding out" of well-performing and highly qualified females and students of color in the STEM fields. This dynamic is not a "STEM-only" issue.

Even when educators working on course redesign get it right, dynamics change. Students change. Institutions change. Leaders change. Modalities and tools change. One of the chief lessons of the COVID pandemic was that change happens—sometimes really fast. These changes mean that even the best course redesign plans must be revisited and revised on a consistent basis. As Dr. Shirley Malcom—who for years served as the director of the American Association for the Advancement of Science's Division of Human Resources and Education—once told me, "Drew, fixed don't stay fixed." Course redesign work is never done.

Because of this, institutions must plan for the constant nature of course redesign work. After all, it is not called "continuous quality improvement" for nothing! If asked for a very specific answer to what faculty and staff need to do with their plans once they have initially implemented them, my best answer is a hearty, "It depends." It depends on the institutional situation and the lived experience of faculty and students in the redesigned sections. In short, the third phase of the work is all about context and continuous improvement.

In general, the good project management, evaluation, and faculty development structures that helped get the plans launched will sustain and allow for successful change and scaling of the plans during the third phase and beyond. It is during the third phase that layering of evidence-based strategies can occur. New elements may be added as the initial components are refined. Therefore, faculty should continue to engage with professional development offerings—so that they continue to learn and apply new knowledge to help "fixed stay fixed."

I would be remiss if I did not emphasize the role of discipline associations in this work. Over the past two decades, disciplinary organizations have recognized the importance of teaching to the profession and have responded with support. Whether occurring in the STEM fields with resources from entities like the National Science Foundation or Sloan Foundation, or in the field of history with the leadership of the American Historical Association and support from the Andrew W. Mellon Foundation, disciplinary groups have provided guidance and communities of practice to both learn about and share work. As faculty grow into their course redesign responsibilities, they should be encouraged and supported to "see and be seen" in their disciplinary meetings. Faculty should also look to their discipline-specific publications to learn from and contribute to the scholarship of teaching and learning in their respective fields. I have placed this guidance here, in the section on the third phase of the effort since this is the period when faculty may feel most comfortable contributing to publications and making presentations. But they should "lean into" the conversations about course redesign well before the third phase.

But What Did They Do and What Happened When They Did?

The Secret Sauce—The Most Important Thing in Successful Course Redesign

Invariably, people always ask me to tell them what institutions and/or faculty "did" because of the planning process. In other words, they want to skip the strategy and jump straight to the ends—the tactics. The problem with the "What did people do" question and the thinking that undergirds it is that the question assumes that all classrooms, institutions, students, and educators are the same—that place, space, actors, and time do not matter.

Because your institution is unique, you need to figure out what works best in *your* institutional context. This does not mean you need to reinvent the wheel. Rather, it means you need to learn more about the setting and dynamics yielding outcomes in gateway courses at your institution right now, and then, drawing on the broad body of scholarship on teaching and learning, apply context-appropriate strategies to help *your* students—the ones enrolled in courses at *your* institution—and *your* faculty—the ones teaching courses at *your* institution—succeed.

But if you really are insistent and really want to know what people did that made them successful with course redesign, then I do have an answer for you. It is actually quite simple to share. And here it is.

> *The most important thing that all the most successful people did in their course redesign work with us was to assemble a task force that used evidence to create, implement, and refine the implementation of a plan.*

There you have it. The secret sauce. In other words, the missing piece was an overarching structure to create, implement, and sustain a strategy—not a specific tactic. Now that does not exactly tell you the various methods that people employed and refined as they went through the planning and plan implementation process. But it does tell you what they had to do to successfully identify, test, and refine the tactics.

This gateway course redesign approach is not unique to the Gardner Institute. Since 2011, Purdue University has developed and scaled an approach that helps its faculty learn about and apply strategies to create more active and engaged classrooms. The approach, called IMPACT, combines regular meetings of groups of instructors with technology and instructional-design experts. Collectively, they study the research on effective learning, share experiences, and test out new teaching methods. According to an article about IMPACT published in the *Chronicle of Higher Education*, external evaluation shows that courses taught by faculty in the IMPACT program "generally have higher end-of-course final grades and fewer students who withdraw or earn Ds and Fs." In addition, "(s)tudents and faculty members report greater satisfaction and more active engagement in such courses. Faculty members also say that students are more likely to use effective study habits and demonstrate critical thinking compared with students in other courses" (McMurtrie, 2018).

In summary, a supportive, long-term, institution-wide commitment to and a structure for evidence-based redesign of gateway courses that supports faculty learning and experimentation in a non-punitive way is correlated with higher levels of student success. Again, *that* is the secret sauce.

Some Institutional-Specific Examples

Several of the examples I share here come from two online case study anthologies that my Gardner Institute colleague, Dr. Stephanie Foote, compiled. Titled *Gateways to Completion Case Study Anthology* and *Gateways to Completion Case Study Anthology Volume 2*, the publications are available at the Gardner Institute's website free of charge (Foote, 2021, 2022). For the purposes of this chapter, the two volumes are collectively referred to as "the anthologies."

The anthologies include thirty-three course redesign case studies coming from ten different disciplines plus submissions on the administrative approach to leading change through a course redesign effort. Some examples of case studies detailing specific practices found in the first two volumes of the anthologies include:

- ♦ The creation and deployment of more intentional methods for preparing and supporting contingent and temporary instructors who are employed to teach principles of chemistry at Augusta University (Myers et al., 2021)
- ♦ The implementation of a structure for more effective coordination and collaboration on teaching practices

across varied full-time instructors teaching calculus 1 at Western Michigan University (Mingus, Koelling, & Hernandez, 2021)
- The adoption of active learning strategies to help all students—especially students of color—succeed in college algebra at Eastern Michigan University (Rescoria et al., 2021)
- The embedding of supplemental support, as well as employing the use of exam wrappers, in an introductory sociology course at Georgia Southwestern State University (MacLennan, 2021)
- The use of early and frequent messaging to students as well as more intentional coordination of pedagogy and course policies across faculty to improve student learning and success in principles of accounting at the University of Central Arkansas (Young, 2022)
- The creation of an intensive support program including, but not limited to, learning communities, supplemental instruction, and career programming that reduced racial achievement gaps in pre-nursing courses at the College of Coastal Georgia (Lynch, 2022)

Again, these approaches were successful because they were the outgrowth of an evidence-based learning process that shaped action. These educators used new knowledge to create, implement, and refine better teaching and learning environments.

Examples of Outcomes Associated With the Course Redesign Model

These case studies include many examples of how changes in course outcomes and perceptions of learning were measured over time. In many instances those changes were quite positive and even statistically significant. However, those examples are from small samples and localized to one course in one institution. For this reason, sharing the findings of broader studies that examined the correlation between doing course redesign based on the model shared in the past two chapters and changes in course outcomes—particularly grades—was not only merited but necessary.

My Gardner Institute colleagues and I were fortunate to be able to turn to the same external evaluator who conducted the studies on the implementation of retention plans discussed earlier in this chapter for analyses on grade outcomes associated with gateway course improvement efforts. That evaluator, Dr. Brent Drake, has since joined the Gardner Institute team on a full-time basis.

In 2020, Dr. Drake conducted two different but similar analyses of outcomes for two different cohorts of institutions that went through the Gardner Institute's course redesign model from 2014 through 2020. One study focused on nine colleges and universities in Michigan that did the work over five years (2014–2019) in a grant-funded project supported by the Kresge Foundation—the Michigan Gateways to Completion (Michigan G2C) project.

The other study focused on a cohort of twenty-five institutions from the University System of Georgia that undertook course redesign work with the Gardner Institute over a six-year period. Specifically, USG Gateways to Completion (USG G2C) project occurred over the six-year period from 2014 through 2020. The USG G2C effort, conducted in conjunction with a Strong Start to Finish demonstration project, as well as the Complete College Georgia effort, became part of a broader University System of Georgia effort to redesign the first college year—a broader project called the Momentum Year.

The USG G2C study compared the DFWI rates in redesigned sections of the courses to the DFWI rates in non-redesigned sections of the same courses during the same time period. In total, twenty-nine different courses in nine disciplines underwent course redesign at the ten institutions involved in the analysis. On average, redesigned sections of the course had a DFWI rate that was 1.8 percentage points lower than the non-redesigned sections of the same course (29.3% for redesigned compared to 31.1% non-redesigned). Students receiving a Pell grant had lower DFWI rates in the redesigned sections of the course compared to the non-redesigned sections of the same courses (33.6% redesigned compared to 35.8% non-redesigned). Comparably, Hispanic/Latinx students and Black students in redesigned sections of the courses had lower DFWI rates than their counterparts in non-redesigned sections of the courses (27.8% for Hispanic/Latinx and 36.4% for Black in redesigned sections compared to 30.1% for Hispanic/Latinx and 39.0% for Black in non-redesigned sections) (Drake, 2020a).

This 1.8 percentage point change with 750,000 students equates to 13,500 more students who earned passing grades and continued in programs of study. That is both statistically and societally significant.

In the Michigan G2C analysis, twenty-eight courses in ten disciplines were included in the study. Those courses enrolled over 86,000 students in nine different institutions. Similar to findings in Georgia, redesigned sections of the courses at the nine Michigan G2C institutions had a DFWI rate that was 1.8 percentage points lower than the non-redesigned sections of the same course (30.2% for redesigned compared to 32.10% non-redesigned). As in Georgia, Hispanic/Latinx students and Black students in redesigned sections of the courses at the Michigan G2C institutions had lower DFWI rates than their counterparts in non-redesigned sections of the courses (34.1% for Hispanic/Latinx and 49.4% for Black in redesigned sections compared to 36.0% for Hispanic/Latinx and 50.8% for Black in non-redesigned sections) (Drake, 2020b).

The outcomes in both studies are all from the first term in which course redesigns were implemented. This timing is an important factor. The outcomes show that change is possible already at the onset of implementation if evidence is used and faculty are supported in the course redesign process. But the outcomes also show the reason why educators must continue to be supported over many years—as even the reduced DFWI rates for students of color and students from low-income backgrounds remain vexingly higher than the average for the courses.

Our colleagues in the thirty-four institutions involved in these studies should be applauded—and encouraged to keep going. They have begun. Have you?

Some Additional Thoughts About Leading and Supporting Others in This Work

Before bringing this chapter to a close, four additional points merit consideration as you embark on this kind of work. These points must be addressed early and often during the course redesign effort.

- ♦ Center the Work on High Standards and Expectations

No credible institution or educator goes into course redesign work with the ideas of "lowering the bar," "handing out As," or "reducing standards." Nevertheless, there will be some who assert that this is what the effort is about. Knowing this, you should make it clear at the onset and routinely thereafter that this effort is all about maintaining rigor and standards in courses.

Paul Tough made this point in an article he published in *The New York Times Magazine* in 2014. Titled "Who Gets to Graduate," the article profiled the work of David Laude, a chemistry professor at the University of Texas at Austin whom we met in earlier chapters of this book. While conducting an analysis of student performance in Chemistry 301—an introductory course for chemistry majors that he taught—Laude suspected that many of his failing students did not lack aptitude for chemistry. He felt that "they were smart but confused and a little scared" (Tough, 2014).

Laude also observed that students who failed his course "were mostly from low-income families. Many of them fit into certain ethnic, racial, and geographic profiles: They were white kids from rural West Texas, say, or Latinos from the Rio Grande Valley or African-Americans from Dallas or Houston." They were deemed admissible to the University but had lower SAT scores than their more affluent counterparts in the course.

Using the evidence he gleaned, Laude began teaching a new section of the course in addition to others he taught. That new section was designed specifically for students who fit the profile of undergraduates who previously experienced challenges in the course. Laude gave the effort a lofty-sounding name—the Texas Interdisciplinary Plan (TIP). Tough (2014) shared that, rather than dumb down the curriculum for the students in the TIP course,

> Laude insisted that they master exactly the same challenging material as the students in other course sections. . . . "We weren't naïve enough to think they were just going

to show up and start getting A's, unless we overwhelmed them with the kind of support that would make it possible for them to be successful," Laude said. So he supplemented his lectures with a variety of strategies: He offered TIP students two hours each week of extra instruction; he assigned them advisers who kept in close contact with them and intervened if the students ran into trouble or fell behind; he found upperclassmen to work with the TIP students one on one, as peer mentors. And he did everything he could, both in his lectures and outside the classroom, to convey to the TIP students a new sense of identity: They weren't subpar students who needed help; they were part of a community of high-achieving scholars. "Identical material, identical lectures, identical tests—but a 200-point difference in average SAT scores between the two sections."

In other words, Laude insisted on the maintenance of high standards and higher expectations—for the students he was teaching, and for himself. And the outcomes even exceeded Laude's expectations. Laude noted, "When I started giving them the tests, they got the same grades as the larger section. . . . And when the course was over, this group of students who were 200 points lower on the SAT had exactly the same grades as the students" in the other sections Laude taught. In addition, "the impact went beyond Chemistry 301. This cohort of students who, statistically, were on track to fail returned for their sophomore year at rates above average for the university as a whole, and three years later they had graduation rates" higher than the institutional average (Tough, 2014).

Laude's example shows what can occur when educators and institutions focus on high standards and expectations. Those high expectations should not simply be for the students—they should be for institutions and educators as well.

♦ *Be Inviting and Affirming*

Yes, you should invite caring faculty and educators to participate in the course redesign effort. But do not limit participation to "the usual suspects." Instead, cast a wide net. While you will inevitably get established champions for teaching and learning to heed the call, you may also surface some new persons who can and should be involved in the work.

Remember that committee membership does not come with tenure. So, if persons are, in fact, disruptive to the cause, they do not need to remain in the work. However, more often than not, even the greatest skeptics will become proponents if they have access to the data and are part of the solution. They often become your greatest allies and champions as a result.

In addition, do not set limits on when an educator can join the course redesign effort. If a person learns about the effort later than most or becomes interested in the work after the endeavor is already underway, find ways to incorporate them into the work.

- *Frame the Work as an Opportunity—Not a Punishment*

There will be some who see a gateway course redesign effort as the latest attempt to "fix" a specific department or set of recalcitrant educators. If understood as such, leaders should not be surprised if educators from those departments view the experience as a form of punishment or involuntary service. My advice on the matter is simple—if a specific academic unit or set of educators would rather "eat lint" than get involved in this work, then let them.

Regardless of who is involved, be sure to use the gateway course redesign effort to name faculty as agents of change—not blame them for past outcomes. When doing so, great care must be given to how data will be shared and used. This is a concern even when an institution has many instructors teaching a variety of sections of a specific course. The concern heightens when only one or a few faculty teach the course. Project leaders must frequently make the case that the evidence is being used to further support instructors who teach the courses as well as the educators and units that support those who teach.

- *Make the Work an Institutional Imperative*

Institutions always find the resources needed to support what they most value. If your institution says it values equitable student learning and success, finding resources to support and reward those involved in gateway course redesign efforts should not be an insurmountable obstacle. Leaders can find the financial resources needed to support ongoing gateway course redesign work if they are willing and able to connect the effort to the institution's strategic imperatives. One such example is discipline-specific accreditation.

Discipline-specific forms of accreditation commonly emphasize student learning, success, and equitable outcomes. For example, ABETS—the organization that accredits college and university academic programs in applied and natural science, computing, engineering, and engineering technology from the associate to the master's levels—requires the accredited disciplines to conduct regular evidence-based self-studies that demonstrate continuing improvement in the areas of teaching, learning, student success, and equity. These directly align with gateway course redesign work. Similarly, the Association to Advance Collegiate Schools of Business also emphasizes continuous improvement focused on student learning and outcomes in its accreditation processes.

Institutional accreditation is another opportunity for connecting gateway course redesign work with broader organizational imperatives. The Gardner Institute has worked with many institutions that have connected their course redesign efforts with accreditor-required quality improvement exercises.

Linking gateway course redesign with reaffirmation of accreditation is wise not only for the economy of effort and bandwidth reasons I mention. Doing so also means that the financial and human resources allocated to reaffirmation of accreditation can be applied to course redesign.

While on the topic of federal funding, several institutions have made gateway course redesign the focus of their "Strengthening Institutions" grants supported by Title III or Title V monies. The five-year nature of those grants aligns well with the long-term commitments institutions must make to continuous improvement efforts.

There are many ways institutional leaders can find ways to support gateway course redesign efforts. Linking course redesign with broader institutional strategic imperatives brings not just imprimatur for the work but also the financial and human resources needed for the effort. Doing so also makes sure that course redesign is not just "another thing"—but rather it becomes and stays one of the "main things."

Concluding Thoughts on Facing and Acting on the Truth About Gateway Courses

This chapter has laid out a three-phase approach to course redesign that the Gardner Institute has refined with nearly 100 colleges and universities since 2013. As shared often in this chapter, you don't need to work with us to use the model. But you should seriously consider adopting the approach. As the chapter shows, the model is tried, tested, and correlated with outcomes that advance learning and success for all students, especially students of color and students from low-income backgrounds.

The fact of the matter is that gateway course redesign is hard. Doing gateway course redesign requires that you lay bare assumptions and practices that may be as old and cherished as your institution itself—attitudes and approaches that may very well go all the way back to the founding of higher education in the United States in the early seventeenth century.

One of the chief reasons institutions report an unwillingness to do this work has to do with the cost. In short, whether working with us, some other organization, or doing the work entirely on their own, institution leaders will say they lack the financial and/or human resources to do this work now. While I've addressed resources and costs earlier, I need to do so again here—this time taking a different tact. In short, institutions need to see gateway course redesign efforts as investments in their own future viability. If you don't do this work now, you may very well continue to have the attrition and financial losses that you currently have. Whereas, if you do find the resources to adequately support and sustain a gateway course redesign effort, you may very well experience significant return on the investment.

According to the National Center for Education Statistics (NCES), the average cost of attendance for a student at a four-year college or university in the United States during the 2020–2021 academic year was $25,972. The average cost of attendance for a student at a two-year college during the same academic year was $19,969 (National Center for Education Statistics, 2021).

So, when you recruit and admit students to your institutions, you are essentially doing so under an operating model that says they will need to come up with, on average, somewhere between $19,969 and $25,972 to cover all costs associated with their studies at the institution per year. Based on this, I need to ask one simple question. How can an educator who knows the average cost of attendance at their institution feel good about not wanting to put an equivalent amount into course redesign? Can educators really feel good about asking students to pay for an experience that they know is suboptimal especially if they know their institution won't invest in fixing that dynamic?

While this effort will likely more than pay for itself, there is a more important reason for doing gateway course redesign—something that surpasses financial return on investment and gets at the very reason educators should be working in education to begin with. Examining gateway courses and their outcomes is an educationally centered way of understanding and guaranteeing that the institution is actually living up to the virtues expressed in its mission. Outcomes in gateway courses must be understood as a mirror on the outcomes of the institution at large.

This brings to mind an essay by James Baldwin, "As Much Truth as One Can Bear" (Baldwin, 1962). Describing the responsibilities that writers have to expose the truth in that essay, Baldwin notes, "What the writer is always trying to do is utilize the particular in order to reveal something much larger and heavier than any particular can be." He goes on to share,

> Thus Dostoevsky, in "The Possessed," used a small provincial town in order to dramatize the spiritual state of Russia. His particulars were not very attractive, but he didn't invent them, he simply used what there was. Our

particulars are not very attractive, either, but we must use them. They will not go away because we pretend they are not there.

Baldwin then notes, "Not everything that is faced can be changed; but nothing can be changed until it is faced."

The particulars of the outcomes in any gateway course may not be very attractive. The outcomes across multiple gateway courses may be downright appalling. These particulars will not go away because it is easier to ignore them.

The question is not whether this is true. Rather the question is why this dynamic has continued, unabated, for decades, if not longer, at many colleges and universities across the United States? The time has come for postsecondary educators of all type to turn their backs on arcane understandings about "rigor" and "standards" in academe and the role that gateway courses play in upholding those tired tropes. The time has come to face gateway courses—to change them, so every student can learn and succeed. This is the responsibility of twenty-first-century postsecondary educators. This chapter has provided a rich description of a model that is proven to help transform gateway courses. Now that you know this, and have a model to guide your action, what will you do?

References

Baldwin, J. (1962, January 14). As much truth as one can bear. *New York Times Book Review*, 14, p. 2.

Brown, S. (2022). A conversation with Elisabeth Gruner about her essay, her teaching, and how former students help shape her syllabus. *UR Now*. Richmond, VA: University of Richmond. Retrieved on December 14, 2022 from: https://urnow.richmond.edu/magazine/article/-/22250/ungrading.html?utm_source=www&utm_medium=referral&utm_campaign=magazine-story

Drake, B. M. (2010). *Foundations of excellence in the first college year: 2010 retention analysis*. Brevard, NC: John N. Gardner Institute for Excellence in Undergraduate Education.

Drake, B. M. (2011). *Foundations of excellence 2011 two-year institutions retention analysis*. Brevard, NC: John N. Gardner Institute for Excellence in Undergraduate Education.

Drake, B. M. (2020a). *Overall course redesign results: Georgia/USG G2C*. Brevard, NC: John N. Gardner Institute for Excellence in Undergraduate Education.

Drake, B. M. (2020b). *Overall course redesign results: Michigan/Michigan G2C*. Brevard, NC: John N. Gardner Institute for Excellence in Undergraduate Education.

Foote, S. M. (Ed.). (2021). *Gateways to completion case study anthology: Volume 1*. Brevard, NC: John N. Gardner Institute for Excellence in Undergraduate Education.

Foote, S. M. (Ed.). (2022). *Gateways to completion case study anthology: Volume II*. Brevard, NC: John N. Gardner Institute for Excellence in Undergraduate Education.

Gruner, E. (2022, March). I no longer grade my students' work—and I wish I had stopped sooner. *The Conversation*. Retrieved on December 14, 2022 from: https://theconversation.com/i-no-longer-grade-my-students-work-and-i-wish-i-had-stopped-sooner-179617

Gruner, E. (2022, April). Why this professor no longer grades her students' work—and wishes she had stopped sooner. *PBS Newshour*. Retrieved on December 14, 2022 from: https://www.pbs.org/newshour/education/why-this-professor-no-longer-grades-her-students-work-and-wishes-she-had-stopped-sooner

Koch, A. K. (2017). Many thousands failed: A wakeup call to history educators. *Perspectives on History*, 55(5), 18–19.

Koch, A. K., & Drake, B. M. (2018). *Digging into the disciplines I: Accounting for failure—The impact of principles of accounting courses on student success and equitable outcomes*. Brevard, NC: John N. Gardner Institute for Excellence in Undergraduate Education.

Koch, A. K., & Drake, B. M. (2019). *Digging into the disciplines II: Failure in historical context—The impact of introductory U.S. history courses on student success and equitable outcomes*. Brevard, NC: John N. Gardner Institute for Excellence in Undergraduate Education.

Lynch. (2022). Closing the racial achievement gap for pre-nursing freshmen at the College of Coastal Georgia. In S. M. Foote (Ed.), *Gateways to completion case study anthology: Volume 1I* (pp.

28–30). Brevard, NC: John N. Gardner Institute for Excellence in Undergraduate Education.

MacLennan, J. (2021). Introduction to sociology (SOCI 1101) course redesign at Georgia Southwestern state university. In S. M. Foote (Ed.), *Gateways to completion case study anthology: Volume 1* (pp. 65–67). Brevard, NC: John N. Gardner Institute for Excellence in Undergraduate Education.

MACRAO. (2019). 2019 MACRAO award winners announced. *Michigan Association of College Registrars and Research Officers (MACRAO)*. Retrieved on December 14, 2022 from: https://www.macrao.org/index.php?option=com_dailyplanetblog&view=entry&category=news&id=1:2019-macrao-award-winners-announced

McMurtrie, B. (2018). How Purdue professors are building more active and engaged classrooms. *The Chronicle of Higher Education*. Retrieved on December 21, 2022 from: https://www.chronicle.com/article/how-purdue-professors-are-building-more-active-and-engaged-classrooms/?cid=gen_sign_in

Mingus, T. Y., Koelling, M., & Hernandez, D. (2021). Calculus I (MATH 1220) course redesign at Western Michigan University. In S. M. Foote (Ed.), *Gateways to completion case study anthology: Volume 1* (pp. 37–47). Brevard, NC: John N. Gardner Institute for Excellence in Undergraduate Education.

Myers, S., Spencer, A., Eidell, C., Jimenez-Lugo, J., Carr, J., & Barker, B. (2021). Principles of chemistry (CHEM 1211) course redesign at Augusta University. In S. M. Foote (Ed.), *Gateways to completion case study anthology: Volume 1* (pp. 17–19). Brevard, NC: John N. Gardner Institute for Excellence in Undergraduate Education.

National Center for Education Statistics. (2021). Table 330.40—Average total cost of attendance for first-time, full-time undergraduate students in degree-granting postsecondary institutions, by control and level of institution, living arrangement, and component of student costs: Selected years, 2010–11 through 2020–21. Retrieved on December 28, 2022 from: https://nces.ed.gov/programs/digest/d21/tables/dt21_330.40.asp

Rescoria, K., Ingram, D., Richards, E., Shell-Gellasch, A., Johnson, S., Blair, S., Xu, P., Gibson, D., & Tayeh, C. (2021). College algebra (MATH 105) course redesign at Eastern Michigan University. In S. M. Foote

(Ed.), *Gateways to completion case study anthology: Volume 1* (pp. 48–54). Brevard, NC: John N. Gardner Institute for Excellence in Undergraduate Education.

Seymour, E., & Hewitt, N. M. (1997). *Talking about leaving. Why undergraduates leave the sciences*. Boulder, CO: Westview Press.

Seymour, E., Wiese, D., Hunter, A., & Daffinrud, S. M. (2000). Creating a Better Mousetrap: On-line Student Assessment of their Learning Gains. Paper presentation at the National Meeting of the American Chemical Society, San Francisco, CA.

Tough, P. (2014). Who gets to graduate. *New York Times Magazine, 18*, 26–54.

Young, L. J. (2022). Principles of Accounting (ACCT 2310) course redesign at the University of Central Arkansas. In S. M. Foote (Ed.), *Gateways to completion case study anthology: Volume 1I* (pp. 1–5). Brevard, NC: John N. Gardner Institute for Excellence in Undergraduate Education.

Afterword—
Where Do We Go From Here?

Betsy O. Barefoot and John N. Gardner

Gateway courses are part of both the mythology and reality of the collegiate experience. For some students, they are "the beginning of the end"—where college dreams are met with harsh and unfair circumstances. For others, they perhaps introduce amazing lecturers and new ways of listening and thinking. But as this book has made clear, students' success in these courses is random and often predicted by circumstances over which they have no control.

Since the Gardner Institute was founded in 1999, we have recognized the "gateway course problem" as we have collected national data on first-year students' academic performance across the curriculum. But our intensive focus on this issue began in 2013 under the leadership of the author of this book, Dr. Drew Koch, who had joined the Gardner Institute a few years before. Drew was not satisfied simply to see troubling data from year to year. He wanted to do more than wring his hands—he began to dig into gateway course outcomes data, especially disaggregating findings by race, gender, and economic circumstances, so that, over time, targeted improvements could be made in student performance. And, under the direction of Drew and other members of the Gardner Institute team, improvements have been realized.

As both of us have done while reading this book, we encourage you to think back on your own gateway course experiences. When were they valuable and when were they a disaster? What were the factors that made these exciting learning experiences or, on the other hand, caused you to give up, drop, or perhaps flunk the course. And what can we do, as educators, to increase our understanding of how and why some students succeed, but many others, especially those from underprivileged backgrounds, find these environments major roadblocks to their academic success.

We borrow the title of these concluding reflections, "Where Do We Go from Here?," from the last book written by the late Dr. Martin Luther King, a foreshadowing of the tragedy that we now know was awaiting him. This book describes a tragedy of a different sort: our historic acceptance and tolerance of an environment that foreshadows academic failure for far too many students. So, the question for you is, where do *you* and your colleagues go from here? What do you know about your own institution, the individual instructors who are charged with teaching gateway courses, and successful and unsuccessful methods of instruction? And how would you describe, by race, gender, or other characteristics, the students who succeed or fail in these gateway course environments?

Of course, it's easy to look at this problem and blame the students, their backgrounds, and their prior experiences in education. While we recognize that all students are not equal, we believe that educators themselves should accept responsibility and do everything in their power to reduce whatever inequities result, especially when such inequities are random, based as much or more on the instructor or grading method as on course content.

So, what can be done? What should be done? What must be done? First, the most important and simple (perhaps) thing of all: Talk about your gateway courses and whether there are high levels of failure that result in preventable involuntary attrition. No one can ever fix anything without talking about it. And even discussing this problem in regular academic meetings of faculty is something we rarely do. It just isn't on our radar. It is not of sufficiently high status. The topic is not owned by powerful people who set the faculty meeting agendas. Yes, of course, there are exceptions. We do know that some institutions are indeed talking about, and more than that, actually doing something about this situation. However, this is not a large percentage of institutions nor is it a critical mass of academic departments. So, as a first step, we need to talk. Of course, our discussions need to be based on more than opinions or personal biases. We need data that explore student performance, especially data that are disaggregated in all the ways we have described.

As Drew has made clear in the preceding chapters, we do have ways to address this problem. One way to start is to eliminate any notion you may have that high rates of Ds, Fs, and withdrawals in gateway courses are inevitable, let alone even appropriate and deserved. The late senior higher education program officer of The Pew Charitable Trusts Russell Edgerton often emphasized that *institutions must take more responsibility for student learning*. In other words, the emphasis on who is responsible for student learning must ultimately rest with us, even more so than the students. For example, if gateway courses have been designed in such a way that guarantees poor academic performance and/or failure for many students, we could redesign these courses to obtain different outcomes.

Approaching that redesign process, it can be helpful to reveal to faculty themselves the actual grades they are giving their students (preferably over as many terms as possible so this is not just a cursory examination). Most faculty have at best only an anecdotal sense of how they and their students are performing. It has been our experience that when faculty learn the pattern of grades they have been awarding over time and to whom, they are deeply disturbed and more disposed to rethink both their course design and their pedagogies. It will be important to provide the expertise, consultation, and knowledge we have for course redesign, and simultaneously, provide the faculty development expertise to help faculty rethink and revise the pedagogies they are using and have been using probably since they began their teaching careers.

Beyond the level of the individual course, there is much that can be done as well. We can incorporate redesign of gateway courses into campus efforts to encourage the scholarship of teaching. Getting even more ambitious, we can examine and change the faculty rewards systems to take faculty efforts to redesign gateway course into consideration for tenure, promotion, and merit compensation actions. Obviously, it's important to provide resources necessary to permit faculty to attend appropriate professional development experiences on their home campus and at relevant professional convenings. We encourage academic department chairs and deans to actually talk about gateway course design, improvement efforts, and pedagogies in unit-level meetings and deliberations with faculty. And we should take advantage of reaffirmation of accreditation efforts for selection and implementation of self-study/improvement processes to focus on gateway course redesign (such as the Southern Association of Colleges and Schools Quality Enhancement Plan or the Higher Learning Commission's Quality Initiative).

Finally, make this book a catalyst for you to gather data on gateway course outcomes and talk about these data. What if you organized a retreat around the reading of this book? What if you formed a book club to read and discuss this book and its implications for your unit and institution—especially your students? Drawing on your own experience and our suggestions, we hope that you will recognize the importance of continuing this conversation to the end that gateway courses will become just, fair, and equitable higher education environments that can yield more learning and enjoyment for all students.

Index

Note: Page numbers in **bold** indicate a table on the corresponding page.

academics: Gardner Institute principle 93; myths, perpetuation 63–64; performance (enhancement), belonging sense (impact) 25–26; policies, institutional shaping/enforcement 49; standing 49; support 26–27, 49; third rail 1
Accelerated Learning Groups 11
accreditation 115
accrual 34–35
Act and Monitor phase (G2C)
active learning strategies 31, 90
Adelman, Clifford 9, 68
African Americans: SAT composite score averages 28; students 9, 19–20
aggregate DFWI rates 11
"Amateur in the Operating Room" 39–40
American Historical Association: History Gateways 70, 106
Analyze and Plan phase (G2C) 84, 85–95
Andrew W. Mellon Foundation 70
"Are College Lectures Unfair" 25
Aristotle 51
Aronson, Joshua 42
"As Much Truth as One Can Bear" 117
assessments: standardized 42–43; see also Scholastic Aptitude Test (SAT); Student Assessment of Learning Gains (SALG)
Association to Advance Collegiate Schools of Business, continuous improvement focus 115
Ayers, Edward 70

Baldwin, James 117
Barriers and Opportunities for 2-Year and 4-Year STEM Degrees 46
belonging 9, 25–26, 39, 42, 45, 49, 53, 54; context 49; emotional consequences 42; importance 41–44; learning mindsets 44–53; metacognition 44–53; operation 48; strategy 49
birth rates 31–32
Boyer, Ernest 39–40

Carroll, Stephen 89
Census Bureau Population Survey 28
Civil Rights Act of 1964 76
classism 32
classroom-based alienation 55–56
classroom-based technologies 30
classrooms: belonging 48; issues 53–54
Coleman Johnson, Katherine 49
college: classrooms 41; courses 41; demographic shifts 31–32; experience 67; first year (Gardner Institute initiatives) 96; function 12; grading

policies 65; low-income/ historically underrepresented student access 33–34; students (*see* students)
color line 33–35
committees 91–92
communication strategy 99; creation/implementation 101–103
content mastery: absence 73; emphasis 29, 31, 41
Continued Action and Refinement (G2C) 84
The Conversation 102
convocations 101
cooperative learning programs 11–12
course redesign 85, 95–107, 114–116; action/refinement 104–106; case studies 108–109; effort 104, 112–114; evidence 87–92, 93–94; initial plan 94–95; institutional-specific examples 108; intentional methods 108; leading/supporting 111–116; model 109–111; participants 102–103; plan launch 98–104; planning 96–97; policies 91; practices/policies/ committees 91–92; problem 123–124; process 104–105, 124; ratings 94; structure 108–109; students/educators 88–90; success 106–108; task force 85–87
courses: committees 85, 86, 94–95; content 71; foundational 1, 3–4, 20; grades 100; introductory 20, 25, 75; lecture 25; non-credit-bearing developmental education 3–4; policies 91; redesign 94–95; structuring/ teaching 73; success 51, 67; *see also* gateway courses; STEM; weed-out courses
COVID pandemic 105
"critique with career" 50–51
cross-course task force leadership roles 97–98
Current Population Survey (Census Bureau) 28
curve grading: appeal 27; approach 29; cessation 30; competition 29; guarantees 72–73; impact 72; merit-based 29; myths 71–76; score determination 72; statistical distribution method 27; student performance 72; *see also* grading

Darwinian "survival of the fittest" ethos 62
dashboards, usage 100–101
Das Kapital 50
data: aggregate/disaggregated 87, 88, 100; collection 75; learning-relative properties 52; postsecondary 68
deBoer, Frederik 63–64, 67, 71, 74, 75
demographics 14, 31–32, 43, 47
Demographics and the Demand for Higher Education 44
Dewsbury, Bryan 12, 32
direct student loans 7
disciplines 106, 115
Douglass, Frederick 34
Drake, Brent 8, 10, 20, 67, 68, 110
Du Bois, W.E.B. 18, 34
Dweck, Carol 69

economics: divide 47–48; dynamics 34–35
educators: challenges 78; surveys/focus groups 88–90; term, usage 85–86; work,

promotion 102; *see also* learning; pedagogies; teaching
Emerging Scholars programs 11
equity 67, 78–79
"Equity in Education" (MACRAO) 102–103
Ethnographies of Work (EoW) 50–51
Evans, Annie 70
extracurricular opportunities 55

faculty: content-rich 40; development 49, 103–104; Gardner Institute principle 93; members 68–69; pedagogical approaches 89; reform agents 32; systemic inequity 32; teaching/learning experts 39; work 32–33; *see also* learning; pedagogies; teaching
failure: courses 84; levels 45; range 20
first-generation students *see* students
fixed intellect school of thought 69
fixed mindset *see* mindsets
Flavell, John H. 51–52
Foote, Stephanie 108
Freeman, Scott 12, 71

Gardner Institute 52; assistance 83; founding 122; institutional advice 85; principles 93–94; studies 4, 6; support 70
Gardner, John 33
Gateway Course Experience Conference 52
gateway courses 1; academic support 26; actions 32; completion line 18, 19–31, 33–35; data 18–19; definition 2–3; designations 3; DFWI rates 20; enrollments 4–5,

20–21; faculty usage 54–55; failure 74; foundational aspects 3–4, 73; future 122; grading 26–27; hardship 19; historical contextualization 19; historic data/analytics 87–88; motivation 33–34; outcomes 67–68; race 21, 24; redesign 83–84, 97–104, 116, 124; risk 4; trends 20; truth 116–118; weed-out culture 74; *see also* courses
Gateways to Completion (G2C) *see* Michigan Gateways to Completion; University System of George Gateways to Completion
Gateways to Completion Case Study Anthology and *Gateways to Completion Case Study Anthology Volume 2* 108
Gatta, Mary 50
"Grade Inflation Is Not a Victimless Crime" 75
"Grade Inflation Makes the A the New C" 75
grades: A 75–76; D 6, 75; F 6, 75; I (incomplete) 7–8; W (withdraw/DFWI) 5–14, 20–21, 22, 23, 84, 87, 111; aggregated 100; award 27; curve grading 72; consequences 7; discussions/metrics 4; earning 72–73; increase 75; inflation 71–76; understanding 65–66
grading: curve 30; inequality 26–27; norm-referenced 72; system 65; *see also* curve grading
graduation rates 64, 74
Grawe, Nathan 66
growth mindset *see* mindsets
Gruner, Elisabeth 101–102
Guttman College 50

Harvard 64, 75
haves, have-nots (contrast) 26, 39
Hayes, Chris 27
help centers 26
Hewitt, Nancy 105
Higher Ed Act of 1965 76
higher education: inequitable outcomes 66; institutions 41, 78; problem 35; system 66
Higher Learning Commission, Quality Initiative 125
History Gateways, American Historical Association launch 70
Howard Hughes Medical Institute, project facilitation 92
Hrabowski, Freeman 13

immigration laws 24
IMPACT (Purdue University) 107–108
imposter phenomenon/syndrome 43–44
income: focus 31; importance 10; socioeconomic status 34–35
institutions: accreditation 115; context 107; diversity 33–34; mindfulness 88; questions, usage 89
instructors: Gardner Institute principle 93; multi-year employee status 12–13; *see also* learning; pedagogies; teaching
Integrated Postsecondary Education Data System (IPEDS) 96; retention rates 96
intellect: merit 68; performance 43; prowess 28

Jim Crow era 18, 34–35

King, Jr., Martin Luther 67, 123
Kirp, David 48

Koch, Andrew K. 122, 124
Kresge Foundation 71

LaGuardia Community College 8
Lambert, Leo 96
Laude, David 29–31, 47, 69–70, 112
leadership 97–98
learners: affluent 13; at-risk 26; expectations, increase 32; winnowing 74
learning: environment 44–45; evidence-based strategies 12; expert 39–41; facilitation 30; face-to-face 30; Gardner Institute principle 93; improvement 102; outcomes 35; perceived gains 90; practices 41; scholarship 40; skills 52, 53; transformation 41; *see also* mindsets; pedagogies; teaching
Learning Mindset Scholars Network 49–50
Littler, Jo 27

Mahomes, Patrick 74
majority-minority nation 13, 32
Malcolm, Shirley 46, 105
"Many Thousands Failed: A Wakeup Call to History Educators" 8
Marx, Karl 50
McClenney, Kay 26
McGuire, Saundra Yancy 52
merit-based systems 27–30
metacognition 39; definition 52; importance 53–56; learning skills 53; origin 51–52; usage 44–53; strategies 54–56
"Metacognitive Aspects of Problem Solving" 51–52
Michigan Association of Collegiate Registrars

and Admission Officers (MACRAO) 102–103
Michigan Center for Student Success 71
Michigan Gateways to Completion (Michigan G2C) 83–84; analysis 111; development/goal 2–3; effort 71, 110
Microsoft Project 99–100
mindsets: approaches 69; cultivation 53; deficit 54; description 51; fixed 46, 47; growth 9, 45, 47–48; impact 69–70; importance 53–56; learning 39, 44–53; strategies 44–45, 51; tools 55–56
Mindset Scholars Network 44–45, 48, 70
Mount Holyoke 65
Murphy Paul, Annie 25

National Advisory Committee, assistance 3
National Science Foundation 76, 106
The Nature of Intelligence 51
Nevada State College, Course Assistant initiative (peer support program) 11–12
New American History, use 70
North Carolina Independent Colleges, support 71

Pace, David 39, 40
pedagogies 12, 54; evidence-based 11–13, 41, 78–79, 87, 104, 105; inclusive 12; transparent 12; *see also* learning; teaching
Peer-Assisted Learning (PAL) 11–12
Peer-Led Team Learning 11
Pell Grant 7, 21, 68

Perkins Loan 7
persons of color *see* students of color
Perspectives on History (AHA) 67–68
Pogosyan, Marianna 42
poverty 55, 74
President's Council of Advisors on Science and Technology report 74
Princeton 75
privilege: benefits 34–35; impact of 66; maintenance 62
Professional and Organizational Development Network in Higher Education (POD) 104
project management 98–100
Project Mercury 49
public meetings 101–102
Purdue University 64, 107–108

Quality Initiative (Higher Learning Commission) 125

race: blindness 29; differences 34–35; ethnicity 68; focus 21; importance 10; inequity 18; wealth, correlation 24–25, 28; *see also* students of color
racism 43–44
Resnick, L.B. 51
retention 9, 72, 96
"Role of Ethnicity in Choosing and Leaving Science in Highly Selective Institutions" 45
Ross, Mary Golda 49

Satisfactory Academic Progress (SAP) 7, 8
scholarship 92, 99
Scholastic Aptitude Test (SAT) 28, 45–46, 113
segregation 24; *see also* Jim Crow era

Selingo, Jeffery 18
service sector 50–51
sexism 43–44
Seymour, Elaine 68, 89, 105
Sloan Foundation 106
social capital 10
social mobility 39, 53–56
social networks 42, 55
social reproduction 53–56
"Some Students Are Smarter Than Others (and That's OK)" 63
Sorkin, Aaron 77
The Souls of Black Folk 18, 34
Southern Association of Colleges and Schools Quality Enhancement Plan 125
status quo, maintenance 10–11
STEM: array, goals/methods 89; courses, curve grading (impact) 72; disciplines 68; fields 106; fields, issue 13; workforce, diversity (absence) 13; *see also* courses; learning; pedagogies; teaching
stereotypes: applicability 43; negative 26, 42; threats 9, 26, 42–44
Stewart, D-L 65–66
Structured Learning Assistance 11
Student Assessment of Learning Gains (SALG) 89, 90, 100
Student Experience Research Network 69
students: belonging (*see* belonging); comprehension level 72; demographics 31–32, 44; description 52; distribution 27; engineering successes 64; first-generation 9, 20, 21; Gardner Institute principle 93; Gardner Institute survey 89; gentleman scholar 65–66; graduation 29–30; helping 70; historically minoritized 47; learning 89; low-income 9, 20; messaging 109; motivation 52; population 31–32; possibilities 46; preparation 33–34; reenrollment behaviors 49; shame/stigma 49; success 12; surveys/focus groups 88–90; well-being 74; White 13, 20; winnowing 77; *see also* learning; teaching
students of color: assistance, avoidance 26; degrees, earning 29; failure rates 20; policies/laws 24–25; retention completion rates 9; women 43–44
Supplemental Educational Opportunity Grant 7

Talking About Leaving Revisited 68
teaching: didactic 25; evidence-based 41; expert 39–41; improvement 102; innovations 30; models 30; scholarship 40; transformation 41; understanding 40; *see also* learning; pedagogies
Teach Students How to Learn 52
Texas Interdisciplinary Plan (TIP) 112
Title IV federal financial aid programs 7
Tough, Paul 112
Twilight of the Elites 27–28
"tyranny of practice" 19

Universities Gateways to Completion 71
University of Texas at Austin (UT Austin) 47
University System of George (USG) Gateways to Completion (USG G2C) 71, 110

Wach, Howard 50–51
weed-out courses: gateway courses 1; change 6; climate 14; culture 62, 64–69, 71–72; designations 3; failure/success 64–65; outcomes 67; performers 68; practices 73; predilections 77–79
Weston, Tim 68, 89
"Where Do We Go from Here?" 123

"Who Gets to Graduate" 112
Wilcox, Ella Wheeler 3
Winkelmes, Mary-Ann 12
women of color *see* students of color

Yale 65, 75–76
Yeager, David 70

Ziemke, Niesha 50